THE CROSS
THROUGH
THE SCRIPTURES

THE CROSS
Through the Scriptures

by

F. J. HUEGEL

ZONDERVAN PUBLISHING HOUSE
GRAND RAPIDS, MICHIGAN

*The author affectionately
dedicates this book to his son,*
JOHN EDWARD,
and
YVONNE,
*his wife,
and sons,
David and Daniel*

For I determined not to know anything among you, save Jesus Christ, and him crucified.

I CORINTHIANS 2:2

CONTENTS

Introduction

Part One: The Cross in the Old Testament

Part Two: The Cross in the Mind of Jesus

Contents

INTRODUCTION

IN THE SECOND EPISTLE to the Corinthians Paul the apostle tells us that for the Jews the message of the Old Testament, which they so earnestly read, was a hidden mystery. This impenetrable darkness still exists for God's ancient people when Moses is read. It is in vain that the prophets are read. The deep meaning of the Psalms cannot be fathomed. The book of Isaiah does not yield its treasures. David speaks a language that cannot be understood. The veil upon the hearts and minds of the Israelites will never be removed until they turn to Christ and see in the crucified Saviour their Messiah and King.

"But their minds were blinded: for until this day remaineth the same veil untaken away in the reading of the old testament; which veil is done away in Christ. But even unto this day, when Moses is read, the veil is upon their heart. Nevertheless when it shall turn to the Lord, the veil shall be taken away" (II Corinthians 3:14-16).

In like manner there exists a veil which in a measure blinds the minds of Christians so that they may not see. They are not able to look deep into the glories of the Word, the only difference being that in their case it is both the Old and the New Testaments. It is the entire Bible which to them in large measure is veiled. There has been, no doubt, a glorious sunrise, but there has not been the full tide of a meridian glory. The noonday sun, the astral glow at its zenith, is wanting.

Now this veil is simply that there has never been an unveiling of the central glory of the cross of Christ in all the Scriptures. This is the heart of the matter. The main highways of Old Testament prophecy converge upon Calvary. God had nothing more wonderful to reveal to man. Heaven knows of nothing so glorious — witness the new song of millions of the redeemed about the throne as we have it in Revelation 5.

The very Universe is a poor paltry thing when compared to the cross of Christ. All the ages of eternity yet to dawn will never bring to light aught to rival it. The combined wisdom of the entire angelic hosts can never conceive of anything that could begin to match its glory. It will stand forever and ever as God's Masterpiece. As one writer has said: "Calvary marked the greatest hour in the entire moral history of Deity."

The greatest of the apostles declared that he would not glory in anything save the cross of Christ. Here we have the moral attributes of God coming to their most sublime expression. Here God finds a way to do what, according to the Word of Holy Writ, could never be done, that is to say God justifying the ungodly, and yet remaining just (see Romans 3:26). Here we have God declaring the wicked, righteous, which is the real thought of Romans 5, without the faintest shadow of blame or unrighteousness falling upon His inexorably righteous government.

He frees the sinner who believes on His Son Jesus Christ though he be the worst of criminals, and yet there is not the tiniest hue of a blemish upon His Holy Throne or His infinitely sacred and eternally stainless Justice. Oh, the wonder of it: a Forgiveness which satisfies all the demands of law and which has power to transform the wicked and make him a saint.

Now it is when the Christian discovers the glory of the cross and with Paul determines not to glory in aught save the cross of Christ, that he first comes to see the Bible in its truest light. It is then that he gets the divine focus and realizes what, all across the pages of that vast library we call the Scriptures, the Lord was forever aiming at as His supreme goal. *Now* the pages of Holy Writ yield their deepest and most costly treasures.

The student of the Bible is no longer in the mere antechamber of Revelation as were the apostles until the Saviour opened their understanding that they might grasp what was written of Him in the Law, the Psalms, and the Prophets, and realize why He must suffer (showing them the marks of His cross) and enter into His glory that repentance and remission of sins might be preached in His name to all the nations.

Now the Christian is in a position to see with the clarity of the noonday sun the central message of the Word of God for a sin-stricken humanity.

The object of the following chapters is to unveil the cross of Christ as it appears all through the pages of God's Word from Genesis to Revelation: first in the Old Testament, then in the mind of Jesus our Lord, then in the epistles of Paul, and finally in the Apocalypse.

Part One

THE CROSS
IN THE
OLD TESTAMENT

1

THE CROSS APPEARS

JOHN THE APOSTLE tells us in the Apocalypse that the Lamb was slain from the foundation of the world (Revelation 13:8). The cross was already a fact in eternity in the mind of God, though it had not yet appeared in time. Genesis 3:15 bears witness to this.

Our forefathers, Adam and Eve, had fallen into sin, deceived by the evil one. All creation, it would seem, suffered as a result of man's disobedience, turning away as he did from God to self, to find in himself, as an independent entity, the beginning and the end of all things. One need not look beyond the fact that the earth is one vast cemetery in which unnumbered billions have died, returning (in the physical) to the dust from which man was taken, for proof of the veracity of the Biblical account. Man ate of the forbidden fruit (that is, he sinned) and therefore, as the Lord had said, he died.

What happened in Eden's garden came as a result of a yet more catastrophic defection which took place in an order where time is not measured as it is here upon earth. We read in the books of the prophets Isaiah and Ezekiel that the greatest of the angelic beings, called "Lucifer, son of the morning," "the anointed cherub that covereth," becoming enamored of his own beauty and aspiring to be as the Most High, exercising authority which only God possesses, rebelled and was cast out of heaven, not, however, without drawing after himself into the same shameful way of destruction (rebellion) the third part of the angelic host. So man's sin, also rebellion, followed the pattern of a heavenly (better said, hellish) order. "Ye shall be as gods," whispered "that old serpent the devil."

Now the question was, could it be that God's original plan in the creation of man should fail? Was Satan to be permitted to lord it over man, having deceived him and having brought him under his thralldom? Was there no hope of forgiveness and liberation for Adam's race? Could a reconciliation be affected and the children of men be brought back to God, freed from Satanic oppression? Would God forever be dishonored, His Fatherhood denied, and His purposes unfulfilled?

Was it in God's power to undo what the wicked one (under whose power the whole world lieth, as is the more exact rendering of I John 5:19) had so astutely wrought? Was God to be thwarted eternally as to man made in His image and for the satistaction of His heart of unbounded love?

We have the answer in Genesis 3:15. Man's fall did not take God by surprise. He was not "caught napping" (forgive the expression). Yes, He had taken a great risk, if I may so speak, in making man so great, even after His own image, with the power of choice. But for Him with whom a thousand years are but as a day, though the immediate result was rebellion and grief immeasurable, the final outcome of it all would be restoration. Victory would be achieved. Man would be reconciled and liberated. Satan's work would be destroyed, and man set free.

But it would mean for God a cross. Man could not be restored by a divine "fiat." A divine "fiat" was sufficient for the first creation. But that had been ruined. No mere divine "fiat" could restore it.

Man had made common cause with Satan in a legitimate way; that is to say, in the free exercise of his God-given power of choice. This alliance must be respected. God cannot be aught but just in all His dealings. He could not take from man his freedom of choice. Without that he would not be man, nor would he ever be able to satisfy the longings of God's heart. He must be left free, and he must be turned against the one who had deceived him and who had won his heart.

Satan's work must be undone, but how? The mere exercise of divine authority could not fulfill the exigencies of the case. Man must learn to love God and hate Satan, but how achieve this? Man must learn to hate "self," Satan's ally (as the governing principle of his life), and love the only One who has the right to govern all things. But how?

Only a Man could affect this, and He a fresh federal head of the race. He must be another Adam. He would begin anew. After Him would come those of His likeness, bearing the family stamp. *He* could undo the First Adam's rebellion and sin by refusing the evil one's claims upon man in the full and free exercise of His will and so shatter the alliance. He would choose obedience at all costs and channel the race as its Head into a mighty stream of devotion and faith and loyalty to God.

Genesis 3:15 tells the story. It is the first promise in all the Scriptures of the coming of the Redeemer. The Seed of the woman (only Christ our Lord answers to that) would bruise the serpent's head. The Seed of the woman would bring about enmity on the part of man in relation to the prince of darkness, "that old serpent, the devil."

Now this was achieved through the cross. For as we read in Hebrews 2:14, it was through death that the Son of God brought about the destruction of Satan's work. It was by means of the cross, as it is in Colossians 2:15, that Christ our Lord spoiled principalities and powers, making a show of them openly and triumphing over them.

2

FORESHADOWINGS OF THE CROSS
IN ABEL'S LAMB

IT TAKES LITTLE of the light of Heaven to
see that Abel's lamb, sacrificed unto the Lord, spoke of "the Lamb
of God that taketh away the sin of the world." Why was it that
Abel's offering was pleasing unto the Lord, while Cain's was not?
We read that Cain brought an offering unto the Lord of the fruit
of the ground, and that Abel brought of the firstlings of the flock.
The Lord had respect unto Abel and his offering, so reads the
Biblical account in Genesis. But unto Cain and his offering he
did not look with favor. "By faith Abel offered unto God a more
excellent sacrifice than Cain, by which he obtained witness that
he was righteous, God testifying of his gifts: and by it he being
dead yet speaketh" (Hebrews 11:4), is the New Testament version of that ancient sacrifice.

As a result of all this there looms up before us the dark
picture of mankind's first murder, and that of one slaying his
own brother. "And Cain talked with Abel his brother: and it
came to pass, when they were in the field, that Cain rose up
against Abel his brother, and slew him" (Genesis 4:8). "The
voice of thy brother's blood crieth unto me from the ground,"
said the Lord to the assassin.

Adam and Eve had hardly turned away from the Lord to
their own caprice, partaking of the forbidden fruit, which meant
throwing off God's sovereignty to establish their own ("Ye shall
be as gods"), when crime breaks out within the family circle.
Once "self" is set up as god and becomes the "almighty" force
ruling the heart, clashes of this kind become the order of the
day. It may not break out as when smallpox blotches the face

of man, but there it is, for we read that he who only so much as hateth his brother is a murderer.

Again, we ask, why was Abel's offering, a lamb slain, accepted, while Cain's, the fruit of his own labor as a tiller of the ground, was rejected? Was it the nature of the offerings, one being the blood of a lamb, the other the fruit of the ground, which determined God's approval on the one hand and His disapproval on the other? Or was the divine reaction in the first instance motivated by the difference between the two men, one being proud and given to anger, the other being meek and lowly of heart?

The difference, we must admit, existed. But the difference is altogether in keeping with the nature of the offerings. They are as truly one as light and heat emanating from the rays of the sun. Where there is true faith in God's Lamb, Christ Jesus our Lord, you have not only the ground of the acceptance of the sinner, but also the spring of his transformation. "If any man be in Christ, he is a new creature [creation]." And where "the Lamb of God which taketh away the sin of the world" is rejected (man preferring to trust in his own merits), pride is the inevitable result.

The question takes us to the heart of divine revelation. It can only be answered in the light of the cross. "Without the shedding of blood there is no remission of sins." The entire Old Testament economy substantiates this fact. And, of course, when we come to the New Testament and hear the voice of Jesus saying: "For this is my blood of the new testament, which is shed for many for the remission of sins" (Matthew 26:28), there is no longer room for any uncertainty.

The truth of the matter is that the whole question of the ground of man's acceptance with God is involved. Is it of works, or is it a gift of God? Is it grace or is it law? Is it what man may be able to *do* to justify himself before God, or is it what Another has *done* for him? Is it the cross of Christ which provides for my great need as a sinner, or must I do the best I can, bringing, as Cain, the fruits of my labor, and so just shift for myself?

Thank God, there is a glorious answer to all this. It is "the blood" that speaketh better things than that of Abel's lamb. If there is one thing that is forever established by the Word of God and attested by the experience of Christians across the centuries, it is that the only sure road to the heart of God is the sure and living way of the rent veil. "Having therefore, brethren, boldness to enter into the holiest by the blood of Jesus . . . . let us draw near with a true heart . . ." (Hebrews 10:19, 22).

So we see how at the very dawn of history there are glimmerings of God's masterpiece wrought on Calvary's cross. Indeed there is a Sacrifice which speaketh better things than the blood of Abel's lamb (a sure foundation for right relations and a sure standing before a holy God). But we are grateful for these shadows and figures of Old Testament times which served to herald the Day of the Atonement in the putting away of sins through the blood of Christ shed on Calvary's cross.

3

THE FLOOD – A TYPE OF CALVARY

To SPEAK OF THE CROSS of Christ in the Old Testament and not pause to consider what we have in Genesis where we have the account of the flood and Noah's ark, would be sheerest folly. "And God saw that the wickedness of man was great in the earth, and that every imagination of the thoughts of his heart was only evil continually. And it repented the Lord that he had made man on the earth, and it grieved him at his heart" (Genesis 6:5, 6). "And God looked upon the earth, and, behold, it was corrupt; for all flesh had corrupted his way upon the earth" (Genesis 6:12). Noah is called to build an ark that he might escape with his family from the flood which the Lord Most High had decreed to cover the earth and to wipe out all flesh carrying every living thing to a watery grave.

Noah builds his ark, but the people mock and scoff at the patriarch. It was in vain that he preached and warned, for all men looked upon him as one "gone mad." But Noah continues to prepare his ark of safety.

The hour of judgment strikes and God's Word comes to pass. The waters of judgment fall. "And the rain was upon the earth forty days and forty nights" (Genesis 7:12). "And the waters prevailed, and were increased greatly upon the earth; and the ark went upon the face of the waters. And the waters prevailed exceedingly upon the earth; and all the high hills, that were under the whole heaven, were covered. Fifteen cubits upward did the waters prevail; and the mountains were covered. And all flesh died that moved upon the earth, both of fowl, and of cattle, and of beast, and of every creeping thing that creepeth upon the earth, and every man" (Genesis 7:18-21).

But Noah and his family were safe in the ark, also living things of all flesh, the two of every sort after his kind which God had commanded Noah to bring in to keep them alive.

All this takes us at once to that greater flood of judgment consummated by the Son of God. True, He had not come to judge the world. "For God sent not his Son into the world to condemn the world; but that the world through him might be saved" (John 3:17).

And yet judgment was executed. Judgment needs must be effected. "And Jesus said, For judgment I am come into this world, that they which see not might see; and that they which see might be made blind" (John 9:39).

It was as He turned His face toward the cross and entered fully into the way that led to Calvary, that the Saviour said, "Now is the judgment of this world: now shall the prince of this world be cast out. And I, if I be lifted up from the earth, will draw all men unto me. This he said, signifying what death he should die" (John 12:31-33).

There are two great facts which come to meet us here, both most overwhelmingly typified by the flood which in the days of Noah took all flesh to death. When we gaze upon Calvary's cross and grasp its awful meaning — the meaning for all mankind according to God's Word — these facts come before us. In the first place, He who was made sin (II Corinthians 5:21) — the sin of the world according to John the Baptist when he first looked upon Jesus saying: "Behold the Lamb of God, which taketh away the sin of the world" — He who was made sin, I repeat, naturally took it all down into death. What a burden — the sin of the world. The prophet Isaiah says that the Lord laid on Him the iniquity of us all. It was all swallowed up in death on the cross. The floods of divine judgment swept the immeasurable burden of the world's sin into the awful death consummated by the God-Man on Golgotha's Accursed Tree.

But the flood which took all flesh to a watery grave in the days of Noah is a type of the cross of Christ in another sense. It all comes out in bold relief in II Corinthians 5:14, which reads more clearly in the *Revised Standard Version,* "one has died for all; therefore all have died." This does not rest upon an isolated text. It is borne out in Paul's epistles. It is the backbone of his theology as regards the Christian life.

"For ye died [aorist] and your life is hid with Christ in God" (Colossians 3:3).

"Knowing this, that our old man was crucified together with him [Christ]" (Romans 6:6).

"Likewise reckon ye also yourselves to be dead indeed unto sin, but alive unto God through Jesus Christ our Lord" (Romans 6:11).

As Watchman Nee is wont to say: "The curtain went down on history when Christ our Lord, the Last Adam, Federal Head of the Race (the New Creation) died. It was the end of the old creation."

The flood of Noah's day — a type of God's judgment.

4

MOUNT MORIAH POINTS TO CALVARY

IN CHAPTER 12 of the book of Genesis where we have the call of Abraham, the Lord says: "Get thee out of thy country, and from thy kindred, and from thy father's house, unto a land that I will shew thee." Here the story of the chosen people from whom, as to His humanity, Christ came, really begins. The promise of the Messiah, who was to come, is narrowed down from "the seed of a woman" to a particular race springing from the great father of the faithful to whom it was revealed that in him all the families of the earth should be blessed (Genesis 12:3).

Now we know that all the families of the earth are blessed in Abraham inasmuch as from his offspring the Redeemer of the world, Christ Jesus the Lord, came. It was a daughter of Abraham, the Virgin Mary, who gave birth to the Blessed One whose coming would mean salvation for all the world. Many centuries must go by before the Holy Spirit should come upon the maid of Bethlehem for the fulfillment of the Promise, but it could not fail for it was of God whose promises never fail.

Abraham's faith was sorely tried, for Sarah bore him no son. How could the promise of the Messiah springing from his seed be fulfilled if there were no heir? The makeshift suggested by Sarah, resulting in Ishmael, the child of Hagar, Sarah's Egyptian handmaid, only aggravated matters as future events testified. No, it must be in God's hour and from Sarah, the true vehicle of the Promise. But she had grown old and Abraham, too. Nature's verdict was, "No hope." But the God of the Impossible was in the shadows biding His time.

We read that Abraham believed against hope. He staggered

not at the promise of God and in due time Isaac (Laughter) was born. How fitting was his name, for never was there such rejoicing and such laughter. The child grew to boyhood and then the dark hour struck.

"Abraham," said God. "Behold, here I am," answered the patriarch. "Take now thy son, thine only son Isaac, whom thou lovest, and get thee into the land of Moriah; and offer him there for a burnt offering upon one of the mountains which I will tell thee of" (Genesis 22:2).

There are those who doubt these words of Holy Writ. Could God make such a demand of any man? Would it not be murder of the rankest order? But the story is so fragrant with the glories of another Mount, even Mount Calvary, the Saviour Himself declaring that Abraham had seen His day (John 8:56), blending the two Mounts, Moriah and Calvary, one being a prophecy, the other its fulfillment, that to doubt is to cast a shadow on the veracity of Christ the Lord.

How lovely, the obedience of Abraham. He wastes not a moment. He questions with never a word. "And Abraham rose up early in the morning, and saddled his ass, and took two of his young men with him, and Isaac his son, and clave the wood for the burnt offering, and rose up, and went unto the place of which God had told him" (Genesis 22:3).

Now we need not go into details. There is only one which we dare not pass over. It is Isaac's surprise and remark: "My father . . . behold the fire and the wood: but where is the lamb for a burnt offering?" How it must have pierced Abraham's innermost soul. "My son, God will provide himself a lamb," is the reply. How much wiser Abraham's answer than ever he knew. And yet, dare I say that, when the Saviour Himself, God's Lamb to take away the sin of the world, said that the patriarch had seen his day and had rejoiced?

So may we not say that as the stones of the altar were laid, and the victim was bound and placed upon it, and the knife was raised, that Abraham's grief was mitigated by the knowledge imparted by the Spirit of God that thus it would be in the fulfillment of time with God's only Son, the Lamb who through His bitter suffering and death should take away the sins of the world? "And the Lord said, should I hide from Abraham that thing which I do; seeing that Abraham shall surely become a great and mighty nation, and all the nations of the earth shall be blessed in him?" (Genesis 18:17, 18). True, the reference was to Sodom; but if in such small matters God would reveal his secrets to Abraham (how very small in comparison), with how much more reason in that which had to do with the cross of Christ?

How very significant the word in Hebrews 11: "By faith Abraham, when he was tried, offered up Isaac: and he that had received the promises offered up his only begotten son, of whom it was said, That in Isaac shall thy seed be called: accounting that God was able to raise him up, even from the dead; from whence also he received him in a figure" (Hebrews 11:17-19).

So it is not only Calvary which looms forth in Moriah, the type, but also the empty tomb of our Blessed Redeemer. Abraham's hand was stayed as the angel of the Lord said to Abraham: "Lay not thy hand upon the lad, neither do thou any thing unto him: for now I know that thou fearest God, seeing thou hast not withheld thy son, thine only son from me" (Genesis 22:12). But it was not so when the Son of God was offered up on Calvary's altar. There was no hand that could stay the blow.

"He that spared not his own Son, but delivered him up for us all, how shall he not with him also freely give us all things?" (Romans 8:32).

"Father, if it be possible, let this cup pass." It was not possible that the cup should pass. How else were the sins of the world to be taken away? He that was bruised for our iniquities could not be spared.

5

THE LAMB WITHOUT BLEMISH

WHEN PETER, at the gate of the temple that is called Beautiful, in the name of Jesus Christ of Nazareth bade the lame man rise up and walk, causing a mighty stir among the enemies of Christ, he turned upon them saying that they had killed the Prince of Life whom God had raised from the dead. But those things, said Peter, which God before had showed by the mouth of all His prophets, namely, that Christ should suffer, He had fulfilled (Acts 3:18).

In none of the prophecies of the Old Testament is this fact more evident than in chapter 12 of the book of Exodus. The prophecy appears in symbolical form but this fact makes it all the more real. The chosen people of God were suffering untold hardships down in Egypt under Pharaoh who had resolved to break their growing power by oppression and tyranny. But God had come to their defense and provided in Moses a leader and liberator. A mighty conflict had come at last in which Pharaoh and his hosts were overthrown in the waters of the Red Sea when they miraculously opened for the Israelites, fleeing from Egypt, to pass safely through, but which had overwhelmed the stubborn monarch and his chariots, burying them in a watery grave.

However, the conflict with Pharaoh in which the Lord showed His Mighty Hand smiting with plagues the haughty king who hardened his heart, refusing to let Israel go, came to a climax in the death of all the first-born throughout Egypt, not excepting the heir to the throne in the royal palace. It was then that the Passover Feast was first instituted as a memorial to be held throughout all succeeding generations, the sign of Israel's liberation from Egyptian bondage.

We read of the Saviour's continual going up to Jerusalem to keep the Passover Feast. But the last time it was to be Himself, the sacrificial Lamb, slain, not to celebrate Israel's freedom from the tyranny of Egypt, but to liberate all mankind from the bondage of sin.

How appropriate the symbolism of the Passover when first it was held on the eve of Israel's liberation. It all spoke of emancipation. The central figure was the lamb, which was to be without blemish, a male of the first year.

The orders of the Most High to Moses were that the whole assembly of the congregation of Israel should kill it in the evening and should take of the blood and strike it upon the two side posts and on the upper door posts of the houses wherein it should be eaten.

"And they shall eat the flesh in that night, roast with fire, and unleavened bread; and with bitter herbs they shall eat it" (Exodus 12:8).

"For I will pass through the land of Egypt this night, and will smite all the firstborn in the land of Egypt, both man and beast; and against all the gods of Egypt I will execute judgment: I am the Lord. And the blood shall be to you for a token upon the houses where ye are: and when I see the blood, I will pass over you, and the plague shall not be upon you to destroy you, when I smite the land of Egypt" (Exodus 12:12, 13).

For the Israelite, I repeat, it all spoke of emancipation from the bondage under which he had groaned. And so it is to this day. I was billeted in the days of World War I in a Jewish home in Mayen, Germany. As the Passover Feast was celebrated my good host invited me in to rejoice with the members of the family in the tokens of the memorial of Israel's liberation centuries ago. The same evening with Christian soldiers there was rejoicing of an infinitely higher order in Christ, the Christian's Passover.

The Saviour Himself pointed out that the lamb without blemish of the Jewish feast was but a symbol of His own Sacrifice, He being the Lamb of God that taketh away the sin of the world. Jewish bondage in Egypt was but a shadow of the universal bondage of sin. Pharaoh's oppressive tyranny could only give a faint idea of the awful thralldom of the prince of the darkness of the world under whose cruel sway all men lie.

"With desire," said the Master to the twelve, "I have desired to eat this passover with you before I suffer: for I say unto you, I will not any more eat thereof, until it be fulfilled in the kingdom of God" (Luke 22:14, 15).

Fulfilled it was, the type issuing on Calvary in the great Antitype, the Lamb slain from the foundation of the world, then already a fact for Him for whom time as we of earth know it never was, nor ever shall be.

"And he took the cup, and gave thanks, and gave it to them, saying, Drink ye all of it; for this is my blood of the new testament, which is shed for many for the remission of sins" (Matthew 26:27, 28).

"My time is at hand," said the Saviour. "I will keep the passover at thy house with my disciples" (Matthew 26:18).

But it is hard to say for sure whether the Lord really partook of the Passover in all its details, it so quickly took the form according to which Christians are wont to "remember." It gave way at once, it would appear, to fulfillment "in the kingdom." Who can read the account, as we have it in the gospels and not see this?

One matter more. We read in Exodus 12:46, that as regards the Passover lamb not a bone should be broken — "neither shall ye break a bone thereof."

"Then came the soldiers," writes John, "and brake the legs of the first, and of the other which was crucified with him [Jesus our Lord].

"But when they came to Jesus, and saw that he was dead already, they brake not his legs: but one of the soldiers with a spear pierced his side, and forthwith came there out blood and water.

"And he that saw it bare record, and his record is true: and he knoweth that he saith true, that ye might believe.

"For these things were done, that the scripture should be fulfilled, A bone of him shall not be broken" (John 19:32-36).

6

THE RED SEA — A TYPE OF THE CROSS

ISRAEL HAD HARDLY marched forth from Egypt when Pharaoh, angered over the fact that his slaves had escaped, decided to make a final effort to bring them back under his power. We read that Pharaoh took all the chariots of Egypt and their captains in hot pursuit of the Israelites, who cried unto the Lord. "The Lord shall fight for you, and ye shall hold your peace," was the word given to Moses as he led the host of captives who now breathed the air of freedom.

Israel's position was indeed fearful. The Red Sea before them forbidding any advance, Egypt's armed hosts behind in mad pursuit, and on either side forbidding mountains and desert lands. From the human viewpoint there was no means of escape. The murmuring of the host as they said unto Moses, "Because there were no graves in Egypt, hast thou taken us away to die in the wilderness?" must have cut him deeply. However, as has occurred over and over in the history of God's people, came the words: "But God."

God intervened, causing the sea to go back by a strong east wind all that night, and made the sea dry land, as the Sacred Story reads, "and the waters were divided."

"And the children of Israel went into the midst of the sea upon the dry ground: and the waters were a wall unto them on their right hand, and on their left" (Exodus 14:22).

The Egyptians lost no time in going in after their prey in hot pursuit, but they soon realized the peril of their position, for we read that the Lord took off their chariot wheels so that they drove heavily, crying out as they did: "Let us flee from the face of Israel; for the Lord fighteth for them against the Egyptians" (Exodus 14: 25). But it was to no avail. The hour of hard-hearted Pharaoh's doom had struck. Moses lifted up his rod, in obedience to the Lord's command, over the sea, and the waters returned in their strength carrying to a watery grave the pride of Egypt, Pharaoh and his horsemen, chariots and all. There remained, the Scripture says, not so much as one of them.

"Then sang Moses and the children of Israel this song unto the Lord, and spake, saying, I will sing unto the Lord, for he hath triumphed gloriously: the horse and his rider hath he thrown into the sea. The Lord is my strength and song, and he is become my salvation: he is my God, and I will prepare him an habitation; my father's God, and I will exalt him" (Exodus 15: 1, 2). Israel must sing. There are times when hymns of praise are as spontaneous as breathing.

But what interests us most at this point is the fact that this, *the song of Moses* and the children of Israel, is contrasted in the book of Revelation with the song of the Lamb which as over against the former is called a *new song*. It is the song of the redeemed ("ten thousand times ten thousand and thousands of thousands") whose theme is not deliverance from Pharaoh and Egyptian bondage through the leadership of Moses, but redemption from the bondage of sin under the leadership of the Lord Jesus Christ.

"Worthy is the Lamb that was slain to receive power, and riches, and wisdom, and strength, and honour, and glory, and blessing." "Thou art worthy to take the book, and to open the seals thereof: for thou wast slain, and hast redeemed us to God by thy blood out of every kindred, and tongue, and people, and nation" (Revelation 5: 12, 9).

There is abundant reason for taking the crossing of the Red Sea in safety by the chosen people of God, and the subsequent judgment upon Pharaoh and the strength of Egypt swallowed up by the waters of this same sea, as a great type of the cross of Christ. Revelation 15 points most emphatically to this. "And I saw," says John, "as it were a sea of glass mingled with fire: and them that had gotten the victory over the beast, and over his image, and over his mark, and over the number of his name, stand on the sea of glass, having the harps of God. And they sing

the song of Moses the servant of God, and *the song of the Lamb*
[in the mind of the apostle the type and its fulfillment] saying,
Great and marvellous are thy works, Lord God Almighty; just
and true are thy ways, thou King of saints" (Revelation 15:2, 3).

Paul speaks in I Corinthians 10 of the things that happened
to Israel as shadows and as figures of something far greater yet
to come: Christ and His Church, the true Israel of God.

The Red Sea for the Israelites for whom by an act of God
it was divided, signified deliverance from fearful bondage. Egypt
in the Scriptures ever stands for the wickedness of this world
whose prince is the evil one and who like Pharaoh fights with
unrelenting fury to keep sinful men in bondage. Israel comes
forth to freedom to form a nation of God's own people.

Indeed, a type of those redeemed by the blood of the Lamb,
whose coming out of a bondage infinitely more tragic and fearful, namely the awful slavery of sin, was wrought on Calvary's
cross by the Son of God. The waters are divided by One greater
than Moses whose redeeming work the great Jewish leader typified. It is He, the Son of God, Christ Jesus, the Lord who on the
accursed tree, Golgotha's shameful cross, broke the chains of
the world's awful bondage under the oppressive thralldom of
the evil one who is this world's prince. It was through the cross
that the Lion of the Tribe of Judah bruised his head and shattered
his authority.

But at the Red Sea not only was there a glorious liberation.
There was a judgment. Pharaoh and his horsemen, the pride of
Egypt, were overthrown.

"I will get me honour upon Pharaoh, upon his chariots, and
upon his horsemen" (Exodus 14:17, 18).

"The Egyptians whom ye have seen to day, ye shall see
them again no more for ever" (Exodus 14:13).

"Now is the judgment of this world," said the Redeemer
as He set His face (like flint according to the prophet Isaiah)
to go to Jerusalem to give Himself over into the hands of sinners
to die upon the shameful tree. "Now shall the prince of this
world be cast out" (John 12:31). The cross of Christ does not
only speak of Redemption. It spells doom to the prince of this
world, for through death, the Lord Jesus Christ brought to

nought him who had the power of death, that is to say, the devil (Hebrews 2:14, *Amplified Bible*).

The cross of Christ will be an eternal source of joy to those who accept Christ as Saviour and Lord, for it was through its shame and ignominy that He wrought their redemption and opened a way of deliverance for all who believe on Him; but there is judgment and eternal loss for all who reject the Redeemer and who prefer to remain under the rule of Egypt's king, who is none other than Satan, the prince of this world.

The cross of Christ not only spells redemption for all who by faith receive Christ as Saviour and Lord; it also pronounces an awful doom for a Christ-rejecting world. The apostle to the Gentiles declared the world a crucified thing, which it indeed is, for the measure of the Saviour's ignominy as He hangs upon the accursed tree is the measure of the world's heinous state, doomed by its sinfulness and pride which placed Him there.

7

THE BITTER WATERS OF MARAH —
SWEETENED BY THE TREE

WE READ IN EXODUS 15 that Moses brought
the children of Israel from the Red Sea and that they went out
into the wilderness of Shur where for three days they found no
water. But finally they came upon water only to find that they
could not drink of it, for it was bitter. So they named the place
Marah (bitter water).

It was a sore disappointment for a people whose lips were
parched with thirst and who fainted in a desert land where no
water could be found.

"The people murmured against Moses, saying, What shall
we drink?" (Exodus 15:24).

As Moses cried unto the Lord, so reads the Sacred Story,
a tree was shown him which he cast into the waters; and lo!
the waters were made sweet. And so the children of Israel could
drink to their hearts' content and were wondrously refreshed
and could go forward with rejoicing.

It was at the waters of Marah, made sweet by the tree, that
we are told the Lord proved the Israelites, promising them health
and blessing if they would but hearken to His voice. "I am the
Lord that healeth thee," was the Word which rang in their ears
as they marched forward to Elim where there were twelve wells
of water and where they encamped in the shade of the 70 palm
trees which grew there.

Israel, of course, was not in a position to grasp fully the
meaning of what had taken place. They only knew that the Lord
had wrought for them deliverance as they were dying of thirst.

The chosen people could not know that a marvelous sign had been given to them pointing to the Tree "on a Hill far away." They could not know that their entire history so fraught with meaning for the whole world and all succeeding generations would find its deepest meaning at Calvary's cross cast into the bitter waters of life for the healing thereof.

Why, the apostles themselves did not know until the glorious hour of the Resurrection when the Saviour Himself opened their eyes to see what, in the Law, the Psalms, and the Prophets, was written of His suffering and ensuing glory so that in His name repentance and remission of sins might be preached to all nations.

Who that believes on Christ our Lord can fail to see in this experience at the Bitter Waters of Marah the deep implications of the tree which when cast into their depths rendered them sweet? If you say that this is reading into the event meanings that after all are not there, then the Lord Jesus was mistaken when He said: "Search the Scriptures for they are they that bear witness of me."

To the eyes of faith illumined by the Holy Spirit whose function it is to take of the things of Christ and to make them known (John 16:13, 14), this that took place at Marah sums up the whole of Redemption and wondrously illustrates it.

How very bitter the waters of life have become because of sin. One stands aghast confronted by the awful fruits of sin as at every turn they are made manifest. It is a sickening, horrifying, maddening picture at its best. We thank God for science as it brings its ever enhancing powers in a herculean effort to heal the bitter waters. But it is only a superficial reparation of the ills of men, and never will be more than that.

Ah, but when the tree of Calvary is cast into the bitter waters, there is a sweetening and a purifying and a healing, and a redeeming for time and for eternity which satisfies not only man but God, who can never be satisfied with anything less. Bring guilt, however shameful and however dark to the cross of Christ, Golgotha's awful tree, and see what happens. The most despicable criminal who ever lived would dance and sing with the bitterness of guilt and shame gone forever.

Cast the tree into the bitter waters of the life of one en-

slaved by whatever passion or lust you wish to name, and see
if death does not give way to life, condemnation to forgiveness,
the dregs of remorse to the joy of a child to whom evil is yet
unknown, helplessness and despair to assurance of eternal blessedness, and loathsome slavery to glorious freedom.

Ask St. Augustine; ask Martin Luther; ask John Bunyan;
ask Jerry McAuley, the founder of the East Water Street Mis-
sion; ask John Newton, the author of *Amazing Grace;* ask Tokichi
Ishi, the number one criminal of Japan who before his execution found Christ (was found of Him) in his prison cell. Ask
the Auca Indians who murdered the five missionaries who sought
to evangelize them, numbers of whom have now been won to
Christ through the work of the widow of one and a sister of another. Ask the multitudes of the once "down and outs" who have
been set free by the Crucified, Risen Lord of Life.

Ask the unnumbered millions of redeemed in Mansions of
Light who sing: "Worthy art thou, O Lamb of God, who hast redeemed us to God by thy blood from every tribe and people and
tongue and nation" (Revelation 5).

8

THE SMITTEN ROCK — A TYPE

THE CHILDREN OF ISRAEL march forward from the wilderness, according to the commandment of the Lord, and pitch their tents in Rephidim. But again there is no water for the people to drink. The people thirst, as we read in Exodus 17, and murmur against Moses, saying, "Wherefore is this that thou hast brought us up out of Egypt, to kill us and our children and our cattle with thirst?"

"What shall I do," cries Moses unto the Lord, "unto this people? They be almost ready to stone me" (Exodus 17:3, 4).

The Lord's reply was that Moses was to take with him of the elders of Israel and his rod and come up to the rock called Horeb and smite the rock upon which the Lord, it was stated, would stand. The promise was that as Moses struck the rock, waters would gush forth that the people might drink.

And so it came to pass. The cry of the people had been, "Is the Lord among us, or not?" What more proof could be demanded? A frowning, impenetrable rock, smitten by a frail rod, only to burst asunder with a mighty stream of water, fresh and pure, gushing forth for the famished multitudes to drink until they could drink no more. It was wrought, we read, in the sight of the elders.

No picture in the Old Testament foreshadowings of the coming Messiah has appealed more to the hearts of Christians, eager as they are for unveilings of the glory of Christ, than the Smitten Rock of Horeb. It has been immortalized by Toplady's famous hymn, enshrined in the very heart of Christendom, "Rock of Ages, cleft for me, let me hide myself in Thee; let the water and the blood, from thy riven side which flowed, be of sin the double cure, save from wrath and make me pure."

The thought is so outstanding in the Scriptures that one cannot escape it. The identity of type and antitype is so real that no true follower of Christ has ever thought of denying it. The great prophet (Isaiah the Evangelist, as he has been called), saw the Son of God "wounded for our transgressions, bruised for our iniquities," assuring us that the chastisement of our peace was upon Him and that by His stripes we would be healed (Isaiah 53:5).

The Saviour Himself was wont to speak in these very terms saying: "If any man thirst, let him come unto me, and drink" (John 7:37). "The stone which the builders rejected, the same is become the head of the corner" (Luke 20:17). But the Rock was not only rejected, it was smitten. "For it is written," said the Saviour on His way to the cross, quoting from Zechariah 13:7, "I will smite the shepherd, and the sheep shall be scattered" (Mark 14:27). Jesus our Lord might have quoted from Exodus 17, where Moses is commanded to smite the Rock that water might be provided for the children of Israel. It all comes to the same end. It all points to the same astounding fact: namely, that in the cross of Christ healing streams of eternal life flow forth for all mankind.

As John wrote of how the Roman soldier took his spear and pierced the breast of the Crucified, saying that "forthwith came there out blood and water," adding that "these things were done, that the scripture should be fulfilled," he is so overcome that he loses his habitual poise, his detached manner. "He that saw it," he declares, "bare record, and his record is true: and he knoweth that he saith true, that ye might believe" (John 19:34, 35).

The Bible comes to a close in Revelation 22 where we are given to understand that all sacred history is moving toward this sublime consummation prefigured by the Smitten Rock of Horeb.

"And he showed me a pure river of water of life, clear as crystal, proceeding out of the throne of God and of the Lamb" (Revelation 22:1). The Lamb, we are told in Revelation 5, stands in the midst of the throne, as one slain. Ah yes, the river of water of life, clear as crystal, proceeds from the midst of the throne, made accessible to all who will come to the Crucified, Risen Lord. It is the Smitten Rock, if you please, from which the water flows.

One staggers at the amplitude of the call with which the Bible closes. There are no conditions but one and that is a willingness to come. Every son of earth is invited. Saints along with sinners. None too degraded. None too wretched. None too hopeless. None too sunken in sin. No one is excluded. The entire sinful race is bidden to come. No conditions whatever but a willingness to come. The Water gushes forth from the Smitten Rock for all and forever.

"And the Spirit and the bride say, Come. And let him that heareth say, Come. And let him that is athirst come. And whosoever will, let him take the water of life freely" (Revelation 22:17).

We are all consumed with thirst. The things of earth cannot quench our thirst. Only God can. He bids us come. The water still flows from the wounded side of our adorable Saviour —the Smitten Rock.

9

THE ROCK RE-SMITTEN — AN ERROR

AGAIN THE ISRAELITES as they come to Kadesh are without water and the cry is: "Why have ye brought up the congregation of the Lord into this wilderness, that we and our cattle should die there? And wherefore have ye made us to come up out of Egypt, to bring us unto this evil place? It is no place of seed, or of figs, or of vines, or of pomegranates; neither is there any water to drink" (Numbers 20:4, 5).

Moses and Aaron fall on their faces before the Lord at the door of the tabernacle of the congregation and the glory of the Lord appears unto them.

But this time the Lord's command is not that Moses should take his rod and *smite the rock* that was before his eyes, but that he should merely *speak unto the rock,* the promise being that it would give forth water so that the people and the beasts might drink (Numbers 20:8).

However, Moses and Aaron gather the congregation together before the rock and say, "Hear now, ye rebels; must we fetch you water out of this rock?" (Numbers 20:10). Whereupon Moses in anger contrary to the word of the Lord, smites the rock twice and the water comes out abundantly and the congregation drinks and their beasts also.

But the consequences for Israel's great leader were heartbreaking. He was told that inasmuch as he had struck the rock when he had been told simply to speak to the rock, he would not be permitted to bring the people into the land which the Lord would give them. He would see the land of promise, but he would not be permitted to enter in. He would gaze from afar upon Canaan's lovely hills and valleys and streams, but never would he be permitted to step upon her fair land, "because ye believed me not, to sanctify me in the eyes of the children of Israel," was the verdict given by the Most High.

We know from what we read in chapter 3 of the book of Deuteronomy that Moses' heart was broken. He so wanted to go over and see the good land. And humanly speaking it would seem that after so many years of suffering to bring the people out of Egypt and into the land that flowed with milk and honey, the land of God's promise, he should be the man to lead the Israelites in. "I pray thee, let me go over, and see the good land that is beyond Jordan, that goodly mountain, and Lebanon," was the cry from his anguish and pain. But to no avail.

"The Lord . . . would not hear me," so reads the Word. Furthermore, Moses was told to speak no more to the Lord of this matter (Deuteronomy 3:26). And so he entered not in.

Now the question arises, why? Why was Moses' punishment so severe, for striking the rock in angry fashion, when he was told simply to speak to the rock, with the promise that the water would be given? Ah, there is a great lesson here, and a wondrous unveiling of the efficacy of the Redeemer's sacrifice on Calvary's cross.

Moses had perverted the type. Moses had mutilated the figure. Moses had done a terrible thing in giving an erroneous view of the cross with its once and for all consummation of the infinitely glorious work of redemption. Oh, *no* — the *no* cannot be made too emphatic — the Rock must not be smitten again. The epistle to the Hebrews which gives more light on the meaning of Calvary than any other in the entire New Testament states for us the reason, if reason be needed beyond the Saviour's own cry there on the cross, "It is finished." *"Consumado es,"* as in that beloved tongue (for me) the Spanish.

"But now *once* in the end of the world hath he [Christ] appeared to put away sin by the sacrifice of himself" (Hebrews 9:26). "So Christ was *once* offered to bear the sins of many; and unto them that look for him shall he appear the second time without sin unto salvation" (Hebrews 9:28). The importance of that "once" can never be overstated.

Let no one, priest or preacher, church or ecclesiastic, theologian or bishop, or whoever it may be, dare to attempt to add to Calvary's Consummation. "Nothing in my hand I bring; simply to Thy cross I cling." Yea and Amen. We need but speak to the Rock. "For then must he often have suffered since the foundation of the world" (Hebrews 9:26). No, praise God. "But *now once* in the end of the world hath he appeared to put away sin by the sacrifice of himself" (Hebrews 9:26). Or as in the *Amplified Bible*: "For then would he often have had to suffer, [over and over again] since the foundation of the world. But as it now is, He has once for all at the consummation and close of the ages appeared to put away and abolish sin by His sacrifice [of Himself]."

10

LEVITICUS — FORESHADOWINGS OF CALVARY

THERE IS NO BOOK in all the Bible which clashes more violently with the modern mind than Leviticus. Why these rivers of blood to put away sin? Must the knife of the Levitical priesthood be forever flashing over its victims in expiation of guilt? Was there no other way to deal with the sinner? Could the Lord take pleasure in the death of so many innocent lambs? Does the constant flow of blood as we have it in Israel's tabernacle with its altar for sacrifice, make sense?

If the Saviour had not come as both victim and priest, to consummate the work of redemption on Calvary's cross, there would be no satisfactory answer. But the Bible does explain itself. Now the Lord does make it clear in His holy Word that He did not take pleasure in the blood of victims sacrificed by Jewish priests. (See Hebrews 10:8.) The first chapter of the book of Isaiah is sufficient evidence. "Thou delightest not in burnt offering," said the psalmist (Psalm 51:16). And yet the sacrifices of the Tabernacle, the shedding of the blood of victims without number, was ordained of God. How are we to resolve this seeming contradiction?

It was all for Israel's instruction. She needed to have ever before her the fact that sin is no trifling matter which could lightly be passed over. God's law demanded the death of the sinner. Now if his sin was to be remitted, then justice must be wrought somehow in his behalf. The divine claims of the law must be met. The punishment which sin merits must be forthcoming. If not the sinner then one who could stand in the sinner's stead.

41

It was Charles Finney, the great revivalist, who said that the easiest men to win for Christ were lawyers. They understood the inexorable nature of law. There could be no trifling with the demands of law. If the foundations of government were to be preserved and order maintained, law must be enforced. It was useless to speak of mercy, for law knows no mercy, nor dare law show mercy. The righteous demands of law must be met. If the blow does not fall on the wrongdoer, then it must fall on one who makes himself responsible and accepts the punishment for the wrong entailed.

It is indeed strange that the shedding of the blood of animals as we have it in Leviticus, a foreshadowing by means of fitting types and symbols of the great reality yet to come, in the voluntary offering up of the Lamb of God on the altar of Calvary's cross for the sin of the world, should fail to make an overwhelming impact, laying hold of the heart of man with irresistible potency, *when it is a principle inherent in the constitution of man's nature as a moral agent made in the image of God.* Though a fallen being estranged from God by sin, the remnants are still there. These are echoes of his former glory. The cathedral that he was, though in ruins, cannot fail to speak through the very stones that formed it.

A gentleman testified before a vast assembly how as a boy, his parents having died, he was reared by his grandmother, for whom he was a source of constant grief as he had the habit of coming home from school with things he had pilfered at school: pencils, knives, notebooks, and what not. Grandmother's pleadings were all in vain until one day, according to the gentleman's testimony, she said, "If you come again from school with things that are not yours, you see this needle. I shall put it in a flame until it glows and then pierce your hand."

For a whole month the boy's hands were clean, and then he could resist no longer. He came home with something he had stolen, and grandmother became aware of the fact at once. She took a needle and plunged it into a flame until it glowed and then raised the boy's hand to pierce it. But no, she lowered his hand and then raised her own hand and thrust the red-hot needle through it.

The gentleman said that in that moment he came to feel about his sin as his grandmother did. He said it wrought in him a tremendous moral revolution. He said that he had grown to be a man and that from the moment that his grandmother took upon herself his guilt and suffered the punishment of his sin, his hands were clean. Her sacrifice had made him whole.

Now why is it that when we come upon the same principle in the divine order we balk? We say that the innocent cannot suffer for the guilty. We say that the sacrifices of Leviticus do not make sense. We should be honest and say that we do not like the revelation of the heinousness of our sins which they reveal.

Let us turn to Leviticus 16 where we read of the sacrifices of the great day of the atonement. Aaron the high priest was instructed to take two goats. Lots were to be cast. The goat upon which the lot fell was to be sent as a scapegoat into the wilderness laden with the sins of the people to return no more. "Aaron shall lay both his hands upon the head of the live goat, and confess over him all the iniquities of the children of Israel, and all their transgressions in all their sins, putting them upon the head of the goat, and shall send him away by the hand of a fit man into the wilderness: and the goat shall bear upon him all their iniquities unto a land not inhabited: and he shall let go the goat in the wilderness" (Leviticus 16: 21, 22).

"Then shall he kill the goat of the sin offering, that is for the people, and bring his blood within the veil, and do with that blood as he did with the blood of the bullock, and sprinkle it upon the mercy seat, and before the mercy seat" (Leviticus 16: 15).

Bible students see in this a twofold portrayal of the sacrifice of our Lord. He not only took our sins into the land of forgetfulness (see Hebrews 10: 17, where we are told that our sins would be remembered against us no more), but also tasted death for every man in order that the just demands of the divine law might be fully fulfilled in our behalf.

In Hebrews 13: 11 we read that the bodies of those beasts whose blood was brought into the sanctuary by the high priest for sin were brought without the camp to be burned as refuse. One is shaken to the deepest depths of one's being to learn that it was thus, indeed that it was this way that Jesus our Lord went.

Listen to the words of Holy Writ: "Wherefore Jesus also, that he might sanctify the people with his own blood, suffered without the gate" (Hebrews 13:12).

Little wonder that the sacred writer should add: "Let us go forth therefore unto him . . . bearing his reproach" (Hebrews 13:13).

11

AS MOSES LIFTED UP THE SERPENT

THERE IS NOTHING more meaningful for the Christian in the entire Old Testament than what took place as Israel compassed the land of Edom by the Red Sea, for the cross of Christ, "towering o'er the wrecks of time," appears in all its glory in the incident of the fiery serpents. The Saviour Himself, as we see in John 3 where the interview with Nicodemus is narrated, places His finger upon what took place in the land of Edom, declaring that we have here an unveiling of His cross.

It was a long, tedious journey from Mount Hor (see Numbers 21:4-9) through the wilderness in the land of Edom. We read that the people, worn out with fatigue, famished for lack of water, "spake against God, and against Moses, Wherefore have ye brought us up out of Egypt to die in the wilderness? for there is no bread, neither is there any water; and our soul loatheth this light bread."

Israel should have known by now that Jehovah-jireh ("the Lord will provide") would not fail his people. Had they not seen again and again His mighty arm outstretched in their behalf for the solution of every problem and the supply of every need? How dared the people speak so shamefully of the sweet manna which daily fell from Heaven as the very bread of God for their weary bodies? It was indeed a great sin. Surely, so must be interpreted the word of the sacred writer, "And the Lord sent fiery serpents among the people, and they bit the people; and much people of Israel died" (Numbers 21:6).

Sin *is* a fiery serpent and its sting is the sting of death. It bears within its breast the horror and the pain of its own punishment. If there are those who would so interpret the fruit of

Israel's sin, well and good. The language of Scripture is very strong, "And the Lord sent fiery serpents among the people." The Lord, however you may wish to take such severe words, does let sin demand its heavy toll — "The wages of sin is death" (Romans 6:23).

But where sin aboundeth, grace doth yet more abound. The people came to Moses, saying, "We have sinned, for we have spoken against the Lord, and against thee; pray unto the Lord, that he take away the serpents from us. And Moses prayed for the people. And the Lord said unto Moses, Make thee a fiery serpent, and set it upon a pole: and it shall come to pass, that every one that is bitten, when he looketh upon it, shall live. And Moses made a serpent of brass, and put it upon a pole, and it came to pass, that if a serpent had bitten any man, when he beheld the serpent of brass, he lived" (Numbers 21:7-9).

How wonderful that we may turn to the Lord Jesus Himself to interpret for us the meaning of this exceedingly strange incident. That He looked upon it as a sign of His own suffering and death upon the cross, no one would presume to deny in view of what we have in John 3. That He saw in it a clear-cut foretelling of the healing virtue of His cross, no one who has ever read the story of the Saviour's interview with Nicodemus can fail to see.

"As Moses lifted up the serpent in the wilderness, even so must the Son of man be lifted up: that whosoever believeth in him should not perish, but have eternal life" (John 3:14, 15).

How fitting that the immortal John 3:16 should come on the heels of *that.* For truly the measure of God's love ("For God *so* loved the world, that he gave . . .") is to be found here as nowhere else in all this vast universe, or for that matter, as nowhere else in all the far reaches of Heaven.

Antitype answers so perfectly to type that no further proof is needed. "Look and live," say what you will, is still valid in the domains of modern evangelism. Who that has known the shame and pain, so very mortal, of the serpent's bite (and who, may I ask, among the vast hordes of Adam's race has not known the sting and fallen prey to its subtle charm?) does not know that a look of faith at the Crucified brings the healing touch of God to the soul? Such a one, should there be — and, of course, there are still millions unredeemed — is indeed worthy of commiseration.

But how account for the strange circumstances that a form so vile as a serpent upon a pole should prefigure the Altogether Lovely One, the Infinitely Adorable One, the Fairest among ten thousand, the Lord Jesus Christ Himself? Is there not something immeasurably incongruous here? Could anything more unfitting be imagined? What! A serpent lifted up on a pole to unveil the glories of the cross? The most contemptible of the animal kingdom could never show forth the most Wonderful of the heavenly kingdom! Far better a lily, a rose, a star, the sun, but surely not a serpent?

Truly the Saviour is infinitely adorable, fairer than all the Christian songs could ever tell, but on the cross where He was made my sin and your sin, made a curse (that the curse might be removed), nothing could be more appropriate than a serpent, "that old serpent, the devil" being the author of sin.

Then, too, we read that it was through death that the Redeemer brought to nought and made of no effect him who had the power of death, that is, the devil (Hebrews 2:14, *The Amplified Bible*). The enemy has been judged, his authority has been shattered, his rights legally annulled. The "accuser of the brethren" can no longer point to a broken law. Its rigor was exhausted at Calvary. Sin, which gave the devil legal ground on which to exercise authority, has been expiated. "They overcame him [the dragon] by the blood of the Lamb" (Revelation 12:11).

One cannot refrain from fervent Hallelujah's in the face of so wondrous a work of God. On the cross the prince of this world met his Waterloo, undone forever by the Strong Son of God, clothed in the devil's very likeness, not that there ever was any similarity but only infinite contrast, in order that everything pertaining to the evil one might be taken down into death. "For this purpose the Son of God was manifested, that he might destroy the works of the devil" (I John 3:8).

12

DEUTERONOMY 21:23 — UNVEILS THE HORRORS OF THE INFAMOUS CROSS

THE CROSS OF CHRIST is something so amazing, so wonderful, so great, eclipsing as it does, all the glories of Heaven and earth, that it takes every trace of light the Sacred Scriptures give us to achieve a full-orbed view of its meaning and purpose. Deuteronomy 21:23 takes us far beyond the ordinary, if anything in relation to Calvary could possibly be ordinary, to the deepest depths of its shame, as it takes us to the utmost heights of its glory.

The bare statement of Scripture leaves no room for uncertainty as to its meaning. "And if a man have committed a sin worthy of death, and he be to be put to death, and thou hang him on a tree: his body shall not remain all night upon the tree, but thou shalt in any wise bury him that day; (for he that is hanged is accursed of God;) that thy land be not defiled, which the Lord thy God giveth thee for an inheritance" (Deuteronomy 21:22, 23).

In others words such an infamous spectacle, a thing so execrable, an object so degrading, must not be looked upon a moment longer than the exigencies of the case might demand. The unspeakable thing must be removed at once lest the land be defiled. By no means should it be permitted to remain through the night lest the sun rise afresh and its light fall upon it, revealing it to the eyes of men. Such a thing not only would defile the earth, what is more (and beyond this it is not possible to go) — such an unthinkable thing is accursed of God.

Now what leaves one breathless and, as it were, trembling with awe and amazement beyond words to utter, is the fact that this is precisely what we find when we turn to the pages of the New Testament as regards the body of Jesus. We owe to Joseph of Arimathea an infinite debt of gratitude: for had he not entered boldly into the presence of Pilate beseeching him that he (Joseph) might take away the body of Jesus, the sacred form would have been thrown like refuse to share the lot of criminals, which, of course, Jesus the Lord had come to do, but beyond the ignominious cross there was no need to go.

"When the even was come, there came a rich man of Arimathea, named Joseph, who also himself was Jesus' disciple" (we may add, and the Father's instrument for the protection of the Sacred Form). He went to Pilate, and begged the body of Jesus. "Then Pilate commanded the body to be delivered. And when Joseph had taken the body, he wrapped it in a clean linen cloth, and laid it in his own new tomb, which he had hewn out in the rock: and he rolled a great stone to the door of the sepulchre, and departed" (Matthew 27:57-60).

It is indeed — I was about to say fortunate, but that is not the word — let me say blessed to know that we are not at the mercy of mere theological theories and speculations as regards the meaning of all this. It is sheer madness, of course, taken in the natural order of things. "We preach Christ crucified," wrote Paul to the Corinthians, "unto the Jews a stumblingblock, and unto the Greeks foolishness" (absurd and utterly unphilosophical nonsense, according to The Amplified Bible) (I Corinthians 1:23). Indeed, it takes us infinitely beyond human concepts into the mysterious realm of the government of God.

Let us then turn without further delay to the Word for the solution of so great a mystery. Galatians 3:13 gives us the key. "Christ hath redeemed us from the curse of the law, being made a curse for us." And lest anyone should fail to get the full impact of Paul's word, he adds, "for it is written, Cursed is every one that hangeth on a tree." And where did the apostle find that? In Deuteronomy 21:22, 23, as we have just seen.

So the mystery is now an open secret. It defies human reason, but not divine. That God could be so good as to be willing to leave His throne in Heaven, take upon Himself the form of a man in a virgin's womb, that as a man He might identify Himself with my sin, and with the curse of my wrongdoing, and there upon the cross remove it all by becoming the accursed thing that sin is, only to arise gloriously from the dead that I might be identified with Him, freed from guilt and shame, to share the riches of His grace in the endless ages of His Ascension as one seated with Him in heavenly places (see Ephesians 2:4-6)—such an amazing thing may be to many a stumbling block and even, as the apostle says, foolishness. Nevertheless, this is the Gospel of the grace of God. And so He would have it, "that in the ages to come he might shew the exceeding riches of his grace in his kindness toward us through Christ Jesus" (Ephesians 2:7).

It is all, in a sense, so unthinkable that we have no other recourse but the Word. Men may cavil and stumble and doubt and indulge in theological conjectures, but for waters so deep where the merely human is helpless, we must get our feet on the Rock and listen to God as He speaks in the Scriptures. Isaiah saw it all very clearly, illumined by the Holy Spirit. "He is despised and rejected of men; a man of sorrows, and acquainted with grief: and we hid as it were our faces from him; he was despised and we esteemed him not . . . . we did esteem him stricken, smitten of God" (Isaiah 53:3, 4).

And now comes one of those blessed "buts" which abound in Scripture, offsetting everything of human failure by means of the divine intervention. "But he was wounded for our transgressions, he was bruised for our iniquities: the chastisement of our peace was upon him; and with his stripes we are healed. All we like sheep have gone astray; we have turned every one to his own way; and the Lord hath laid on him the iniquity of us all" (Isaiah 53:5, 6).

We need these strong, clear statements of Scripture when so many pulpits are dedicated to a watered-down gospel in an effort to get around "the offence of the cross." It is still a scandal, an infinitely offensive stumbling block to the pride of man, but to all those who are willing to submit to the verdict of Calvary, it will be for all the ages to come God's Masterpiece whereby He found a way to be just while justifying the wicked, a way to be merciful to sinful man without lightly passing over the righteous demands of His holy law, forgiving sin but not without a perfect fulfillment of the just claims of a government holy and utterly free from aught that could mar, as only God's could be.

13

JOB SIGHS FOR A DAYSMAN (MEDIATOR)

JOB CRIES OUT SAYING, "I know that my Redeemer liveth," and yet he sighs for a daysman who might stand betwixt him and the Most High, one who could lay his hand upon both God and man and bring them together (see Job 9:33).

No one, save of course the Son of God, was ever more severely tried than Job. It was because Satan was given permission to strip him of all that he had, having been the richest man of his day — lands, cattle, sons and daughters, health, all was taken from him. God had said that there was none like him in the earth, a perfect and an upright man who feared God and rejected evil. But Satan contradicted the Lord, affirming that Job's loyalty was a fictitious thing and that it was all a mere convenience.

"Doth Job fear God for nought? Hast thou not made a hedge about him, and about his house, and about all that he hath on every side? thou hast blessed the work of his hands, and his substance is increased in the land," is Satan's complaint. In other words the charge is that the Lord had really paid a high price for Job's devotion. The evil one, as it were, dares the Lord to give him (the devil) the chance to strip him (Job) clean of all that he has, lands, cattle, children, health, stating that the result would be Job cursing God to His face.

The Most High accepts the challenge. Satan is given a free hand. The blows begin to fall and they do not cease until the great patriarch, reduced to the deepest depths of poverty, smitten with sore boils from the sole of his feet unto his crown, sits down among the ashes to scrape his pestilential skin with a potsherd. His wife goes under, so to speak, and bids him curse God and die.

But Job, so reads the Sacred Scripture, sinned not nor charged God foolishly. What aggravated matters beyond measure was the fact that Job's so-called friends, who came to console (?) him with their meagre theology, press home to Job the fact that there must be sin in the camp else the patriarch would not be in such a state. If Job would only confess it all to the Lord and straighten out accounts, his sin would be forgiven and all would be well.

Job defends himself in royal fashion. Poor man, it was only natural that he should cling to his integrity and fight to the bitter end to prove that his hands were clean — it was all that he had left. And yet in the midst of his wretchedness, his sorrow over his losses, his diseased body covered with boils, his friends' accusations that something terribly rotten needed to be confessed, Job though defending his integrity and declaring his innocence, has moments of high illumination in which he sees his inherent sinfulness. "If I justify myself, mine own mouth shall condemn me: if I say, I am perfect, it shall also prove me perverse" (Job 9:20). The great patriarch withal knows himself (what man does know this) to be a sinner, though he felt that the charges of his friends must be denied.

"If I be wicked [*since I am wicked* is the thought], why then labour I in vain?" Job goes on to say. "If I wash myself with snow water [nothing cleaner], and make my hands never so clean; yet shalt thou plunge me in the ditch, and mine own clothes shall abhor me. For he [the Lord] is not a man, as I am, that I should answer him, and we should come together in judgment" (Job 9:29-32).

And now we come to what we are aiming at. Job cries out for a daysman (mediator). "Neither is there any daysman betwixt us, that might lay his hand upon us both" (Job 9:33).

There is no more beautiful flowering of the Messianic hope which throughout the Old Testament takes such varied forms and appears in such significant ways, as this. The crucible has been heated beyond measure, and in the midst of the fiery trial this is what comes to the surface: man needs a daysman (umpire, mediator) who can put his hand upon him and God and so bring them together. But this is not possible, for the daysman, in order to effectively fulfill his office, needs must be both God and man. He must be able to represent God perfectly — only God can do that. He must be able to represent man perfectly— only man can do that. Who but God fully knows what the claims of the divine government are? Only man knows what it is to suffer as men suffer and are tempted as men can be. How bring the "all" of man in perfect harmony and reconciliation with the "all" of God?

Job realizes the immensity of the problem. Who could ever speak for God in the full measure of understanding and authority, but God? Who could ever speak for man in the fullest possible appreciation of his need, but man?

Well, thank God, we know the answer. It is none other than Bethlehem's manger. It is the Blessed One who trod the dusty roads of Galilee, "tempted in all points like as we," the One who met the subtle onslaughts of the prince of this world there in the wilderness. It is the One who sat beside the well and asked for a cool drink of water to quench His thirst. It is the One who was betrayed by one who had shared His most intimate thought and feeling. It is the One despised and rejected by men, for He refused to go along with them in their bigotry and their prejudices.

And here it is that we come to the other side of the picture — the divine. We said that the Mediator would have to be God, for God alone knows what the claims of His righteous government are, and how they can be satisfied. And that meant the cross. "Once in the end of the world hath he appeared to put away sin by the sacrifice of himself" (Hebrews 9:26). "For it pleased the Father that in him [Christ] should all fulness dwell; and, *having made peace through the blood of his cross,* by him to reconcile all things unto himself; by him, I say, whether they be things in earth, or things in heaven" (Colossians 1:19, 20).

The problem—truly of infinite dimensions—has been solved. There was One great enough to measure up to the exigencies of the case. We said that only God could fulfill the need. And so it was: "Great is the mystery of godliness: God was manifest in the flesh" (I Timothy 3:16). We were saying that only a man, another Adam, federal head of the race (one tempted in all points like as we), could effect the transformation. And so it was that the Strong Son of God became the Son of Man. And now we, if we will but believe and appropriate all that is ours in our Adorable Saviour, may become heirs of God, joint heirs with Christ. "For there is one God, and one mediator between God and men, the man Christ Jesus" (I Timothy 2:5).

14

PSALM 2 TAKES US TO CALVARY

WHEN THE RISEN CHRIST appeared to the disciples, we read that He opened their minds so that they might understand the Scriptures, how that what was written of Him in the law, the Psalms, and the Prophets must be fulfilled (Luke 24:44, 45). It is in the Psalms that the Messianic Hope comes to a consummate expression. We shall not attempt a complete appraisal, but only look into those which bring the cross before us.

Paul in his sermon at Antioch of Pisidia places his finger, so to speak, on the second Psalm, the seventh verse, declaring that we have its fulfillment in Jesus our Lord (Acts 13:33). Hebrews 1:5 gives us further confirmation of the fact that Psalm 2 is one of the most outstanding passages of the Old Testament.

The Psalm opens with the kings of the earth setting themselves against the Lord's anointed, and the rulers taking counsel, saying: "Let us break their bands asunder, and cast away their cords from us." Centuries later as the cry, "Crucify him, crucify him," was heard, "Let his blood be upon us and upon our children," it was no longer prophecy, but stark reality. The bands which tied the Jews with this One (for them a pretender king) and the cords which bound them were plucked asunder with such a fury and such a boundless rage that for all the ensuing years Israel's "No!" to the claims of Christ has stood out as history's most emphatic denial of One who would be king of whatever people or nation.

But Psalm 2 not only spoke of Messiah's rejection, nailed as He was to the shameful tree; here we also have the Resurrection, yea, and also Messiah's Ascension faithfully foretold.

Nothing is lacking. Israel's sweet singer, David (whose Son, Messiah as to the flesh claimed to be) looked far down the years to the universal reign of her crucified King, risen and glorified to hold sway over all the earth. "He that sitteth in the heavens shall laugh: the Lord shall have them in derision. Then shall he speak unto them in his wrath, and vex them in his sore displeasure. Yet have I set my king upon my holy hill of Zion. I will declare the decree: the Lord hath said unto me, Thou art my Son, this day have I begotten thee. Ask of me, and I shall give thee the heathen for thine inheritance, and the uttermost parts of the earth for thy possession" (Psalm 2:4-8).

Whereupon the psalmist takes upon himself the role of the preacher who proclaims the everlasting Gospel of the Lord Jesus Christ, and speaks saying, "Be wise now therefore, O ye kings: be instructed, ye judges of the earth. Serve the Lord with fear, and rejoice with trembling. Kiss the Son . . . blessed are all they who put their trust in him" (Psalm 2:10-12).

Little wonder that Christians, as Peter tells us, rejoice with joy unspeakable and full of glory. Little wonder that the enemies of the Christians of Paul's day found that nothing could quench the fire of their enthusiasm and devotion: neither threats, nor imprisonments, nor stonings, nor the lions of Nero's circus, nor anything else! The kiss of pardon and reconciliation offered to all men everywhere through Calvary's cross can turn the night of the despair of earth's most wretched son into the day of an everlasting bliss whose joy knows no bounds. Has he not been bidden to kiss the Son?

But why speak of wrath? "Kiss the Son, lest he be angry, and ye perish from the way, when his wrath is kindled but a little" (Psalm 2:12). Why do we read that upon the occasion of the return of Christ to judge and reign as, of course, He must, that the kings of the earth, and the great men, and the rich men, and the chief captains, and the mighty men, and every bondman, and every freeman, shall hide themselves in the dens and rocks of the mountains, and shall call on the mountains to fall on them in order to hide them from him that sitteth on the throne and from the wrath of the Lamb? (Revelation 6:15-17).

The reason is not hard to find. It is to be found, strange to say, in the cross of Christ which is not only the fountainhead of forgiveness and peace and reconciliation and eternal life, but also of judgment and eternal loss. For if I spurn the gift of God's love provided at so great a cost, Christ Himself having been willing to become my sin (see II Corinthians 5:21), that I might be made the righteousness of God in Him, then, of course, I must answer for my sins. Judgment and death (the wages of sin) await me.

There is but one refuge, the wounded side of the Crucified, in which all who will, may hide. The Son is waiting. He offers you His kiss of pardon. He can do no more. Beyond Calvary's cross, God cannot go. He exhausted all His love, and wisdom, and power at Calvary for the liberation of the sinner, who needs but kiss the Son to be saved.

15

THE PSALM OF THE CRUCIFIXION

THE TWENTY-SECOND PSALM has been right-fully called the Crucifixion Psalm. Here the prophet takes us deep into the horrors of the cross while at the same time we are made to see the fruits of the Redeemer's passion in the establishment of His kingdom among men. Even though the Psalm should be the expression of a personal anguish on the part of David, crying out and saying, "My God, my God, why hast thou forsaken me?" this in no wise invalidates the claim. All Old Testament foreshadowings of the Coming Messiah have their roots in what seem to be purely historical circumstances in the life of the chosen people.

We have the authority of John, the beloved disciple, who in describing what took place at Calvary, says that the soldiers casting lots for the Saviour's robe said, "Let us not rend it," fulfilling what in Psalm 22 was written: "They part my garments among them, and cast lots upon my vesture." The cry of the dying Son of God, "I thirst," the apostle says had been foretold when the psalmist exclaimed, saying: "My tongue cleaveth to my jaws; and thou hast brought me into the dust of death."

A more exact expression of the Redeemer's thoughts and feeling during the awful six hours on the cross of Calvary could not be found in all the Scriptures (they bear witness of me, said Jesus) than what we have in Psalm 22.

I am a worm, and no man; a reproach of men, and despised of the people. All they that see me laugh me to scorn: they shoot out the lip, they shake the head, saying,
He trusted on the Lord that he would deliver him: let him deliver him, seeing he delighted in him . . .

Many bulls have compassed me: strong bulls of Bashan have beset me round.

They gaped upon me with their mouths, as a ravening and a roaring lion.

I am poured out like water, and all my bones are out of joint: my heart is like wax; it is melted in the midst of my bowels . . .

For dogs have compassed me: the assembly of the wicked have inclosed me; they pierced my hands and my feet.

I may tell all my bones: they look and stare upon me.

They part my garments among them, and cast lots upon my vesture.

Ah, we may be sure that never had the devil as the "roaring lion" that he is, closed in on any man with such a rage. Never was he so determined to wreck a soul. Without a doubt he threw in all that the hellish hosts of the kingdom of darkness have at their disposal. The Saviour Himself said that this was the hour of the power of darkness, and that Satan would come but would find nothing in Him. A more glorious *beginning* and a more ignominious *ending* (seemingly) was never known in the history of man. Who would believe on such a Saviour? Did not the Scripture itself say that one hanged thus on a tree was accursed of God?

But, oh, how mistaken the devil was. Why, that cross was to be the means of the supreme revelation of the glory of God. Here the moral attributes of God were to come to their sublimest manifestation. The truth of the matter is that here where Satan did his worst, Jesus did His best. Evil Haman was hanged on the gallows he had erected for Mordecai the just. Here it was that the adversary was stripped of his authority. For did not the Saviour bear in His body on the cross the sins of all men, thus annulling the rights of the evil one to accuse and enslave them? See Revelation 12:10, 11 — "Now is come salvation, and strength, and the kingdom of our God, and the power of his Christ: for the accuser of our brethren is cast down, which accused them before our God day and night. And they overcame him by the blood of the Lamb . . . ."

The twenty-second Psalm does not close without proclaiming this fact: "They shall come, and shall declare his righteousness unto a people that shall be born, that he hath done this" (Psalm 22:31). It is declared that all the ends of the world shall remember and turn to the Lord, and all the kindreds of the nations shall worship Him. "The meek," so it reads, "shall eat and be satisfied: they shall praise the Lord that seek him: your heart shall live for ever" (Psalm 22:26).

"I am the living bread which came down from heaven: if any man eat of this bread he shall live for ever: and the bread that I will give is my flesh, which I will give for the life of the world. . . . Verily, verily, I say unto you, Except ye eat the flesh of the Son of man, and drink his blood, ye have no life in you. Whoso eateth my flesh and drinketh my blood, hath eternal life; and I will raise him up at the last day. For my flesh is meat indeed, and my blood is drink indeed" (John 6:51-55).

In this fashion our Saviour, the Lord Jesus Christ, links up His cross and the victory wrought on Calvary, with the glorious life of the ages which He imparts to Christians.

16

ISAIAH 53 — EVEREST OF HOPE

NOWHERE IN THE whole realm of prophecy does Calvary's cross loom before us in such bold relief as in Isaiah 53. Had the prophet stood at the foot of the cross he could not have given to the world a more exact account of what took place. One would have thought that he had written Romans 5 long before Paul's day.

Solomon, who became a missionary to Brazil, was born of Jewish parents in Austria. One day, as a boy, he went to his father and asked of whom the prophet spoke in Isaiah 53. For an answer, he was given a blow in the mouth. (How different Philip the Evangelist's reply when asked this same question by the Ethiopian prince, Acts 8.) Why such anger? The boy Solomon could be insinuating that there was a bare possibility that the prophet spoke of Jesus. Later as a young man, Solomon went to London to work, where one day he was invited to a meeting of Hebrew Christians, the theme of the gathering being Isaiah 53. He thought he would attend the meeting to see what answer these fellow Jews had to this question. He had not forgotten his father's answer.

The result was Solomon's conversion. He later married in the U.S.A. and then answered God's call to Brazil where he and his wife have spent their years preaching the Gospel of the Lord Jesus Christ.

Now Philip, the evangelist, lost no time in taking the Ethiopian prince who once asked this same question as he read Isaiah 53, to Jesus. "Then Philip opened his mouth and began at the same scripture, and preached unto him Jesus" (Acts 8:

35). Who else was wounded for our transgressions? Who was it that was bruised for our iniquities? Upon whom was the chastisement of our peace, if not upon Jesus Christ, the Lord? Who was it that was brought as a Lamb to the slaughter, and yet opened not His mouth? Who was it that was stricken for the transgression of God's people? If it is not by the stripes of Jesus our Lord that we are healed, then pray tell me by whose?

Now we know how these burning questions were answered by the Saviour, and later by the apostles. If Jesus does not answer to Isaiah 53, the sun does not answer to light, nor the moon to night. Why the many stripes at Pilate's bloody post? Why the soldier's spear piercing the Saviour's breast? Why the Saviour's Word: "This is my blood of the new testament, which is shed for many for the remission of sins" (Matthew 26:28)? Was Peter mistaken when he wrote in the language of Isaiah, "by whose stripes we are healed" (I Peter 2:24)?

One is overwhelmed with the prophet's precision as he writes: "He made his grave with the wicked, and with the rich in his death; because he had done no violence, neither was any deceit in his mouth" (Isaiah 53:9). Did He not make His grave with the wicked, crucified, as He was, between two thieves? Did He not lie in the tomb of rich Joseph of Arimathea, identified with the rich in His death, as said the prophet?

Oh, how very moving as we read:

> Yet it pleased the Lord to bruise him; he hath put him to grief: when thou shalt make his soul an offering for sin, he shall see his seed, he shall prolong his days, and the pleasure of the Lord shall prosper in his hand. He shall see of the travail of his soul, and shall be satisfied: by his knowledge shall my righteous servant justify many; for he shall bear their iniquities. Therefore will I divide him a portion with the great, and he shall divide the spoil with the strong; because he hath poured out his soul unto death: and he was numbered with the transgressors; and he bare the sin of many, and made intercession for the transgressors (Isaiah 53).

Let all those, and their number seems to be multiplying these days, who curl the lip with scorn, and look with disdain upon the great Biblical doctrine of Blood Atonement (the central doctrine of the Scriptures), who feel satisfied with their own religious efforts, and who are sure that they will enter in through the pearly gates with some form of law as their guide, turn to Isaiah 53. The prophet will immediately take them to the mount called Calvary, and point them to the crucified Saviour, and say: "By His stripes we are healed; the chastisement of our peace was upon Him."

Let all those who, having tried many physicians, are still no better, whose wounds defy all earthly balms, and whose aching existence, in spite of fortune and fame, is still void of any true meaning, open the Book to Isaiah 53, where they will find that though like sheep we have all gone astray and turned every one to our own way, yet the Lord laid on Him the iniquity of us all, and therefore we may be free from galling guilt complexes, and may find immeasurable security in the Good Shepherd's fold.

Let all those who feel that there is no hope with so great a burden of sin listen to the prophet as he points to the Lamb of God who takes away the sin of the world. Let them heed God's Word: "My righteous servant shall justify many, for he shall bear their iniquities."

17

WHAT ARE THESE WOUNDS?

WE SHALL NOT ATTEMPT to exhaust the Old Testament in its foreshadowings of the cross of Christ. However, there is a word in the book of the prophet Zechariah which we must not fail to observe ere we go on into the New Testament.

It is a Messianic passage which the Saviour Himself took upon His lips the night of His betrayal when He washed the disciples' feet and spoke of the shedding of His blood for the remission of sins. "All ye shall be offended because of me this night: for it is written, I will smite the shepherd, and the sheep of the flock shall be scattered abroad" (Matthew 26:31).

But this is not all. The prophet said more. He refers to the Father as saying: "Awake, O sword, against my shepherd, and against the man that is my fellow . . . smite the shepherd . . . ."

How are we to interpret this amazing utterance from the mouth of the Most High? Are we to draw the conclusion to which some have come, that Jesus our Lord through His bitter suffering and death appeased the wrath of Almighty God and so wrought deliverance for sinful man? The text seems to bear out the idea. But such an interpretation does violence to Scripture taken as a whole. Such divisions do not exist in the Three Persons of the Godhead. John 3:16 tells the story. "God so *loved* the world that he gave his only begotten Son . . . ." The Saviour did not appease the wrath of God by means of the cross; He *revealed* the righteous wrath of God as Paul tells us in Romans 1:18. "For the wrath of God is revealed from heaven against all ungodliness and unrighteousness of men . . . ." Yes, there was wrath, the wrath of God against sin as we have it in Hebrews

9:26: "He has once for all at the consummation and close of the ages appeared to put away and abolish sin by His sacrifice of Himself" (*The Amplified Bible*). Let us not forget that the old man (the old, unrenewed nature, the source of all sin) was nailed to the cross with Christ.

But, returning to the prophet, we come to that heart-rending question which we are told God's ancient people will utter upon the return of their rejected King, the crucified Messiah, saying: "What are these wounds in thine hands?" the answer being, "Those with which I was wounded in the house of my friends" (Zechariah 13:6).

Ah yes, "They shall look upon me," saith the Lord, "whom they have pierced, and they shall mourn for him, as one mourneth for his only son, and shall be in bitterness for him, as one that is in bitterness for his firstborn" (Zechariah 12:10).

But, let us not overlook the fact that mourning, perhaps of another kind, is due the household of faith, us Christians, who by our ecclesiastical rivalries, and strife, and divisions, have so wounded the body of Christ, the Church, which the Saviour so earnestly prayed might be one, even as He and the Father are one. What about the wound in our Lord's body because of our racial discriminations, our lack of love for those of the body who perhaps are less fortunate?

The prophet does not fail to come to the heart of the matter: "In that day," he says, "there shall be a fountain opened . . . for sin and for uncleanness" (Zechariah 13:1). "And it shall be in that day, that living waters shall go out from Jerusalem" (Zechariah 14:8). "And I will pour upon the house of David, and upon the inhabitants of Jerusalem, the spirit of grace and of supplication: and they shall look upon me whom they have pierced . . ." (Zechariah 12:10).

Joseph Rabinowitz was a Russian Jew who traveled to distant lands in search of a haven of rest, a place of security where persecuted Jews might find peace and happiness. Among the countries visited was the Holy Land, once the abode of his people now scattered over the face of the earth. One day he sat on the Mount of Olives and opened his Bible (the Old Testament). His eye fell upon Zechariah 12:10, "and they shall look upon me whom they have pierced." In that instant it befell him as another Jew many years before on the road to Damascus. The Lord spoke to him and he realized in that moment that Jesus was indeed the Christ, the promised Messiah.

Joseph Rabinowitz returned to Russia to spend the remainder of his days preaching the Gospel to his people. His favorite approach was this: We Jews are like a farmer on the way to market with the fruits of his land. A wheel has come off his wagon and he is looking for the wheel up ahead on the road. He will never find it there. He must turn *back to find the wheel*. We Jews are looking ahead on life's way for the Messiah, who we think has not yet appeared. It is a great mistake. We must turn back to the One whom we rejected, to Jesus — He is the Christ, the Messiah. It is the One whom we pierced who alone can save us.

Part Two

THE CROSS
IN THE
MIND OF JESUS

18

BEHOLD THE LAMB OF GOD

JOHN THE BAPTIST might have said, "Behold your King." He might have cried, "Behold the promised Messiah." He might have exclaimed, "Behold the Son of God." He certainly could have said, "Behold the Prophet — now we shall be taught the way of God, the perfect law of the Kingdom." But this would not have expressed the true genius of the Scriptures. The supreme note of Holy Writ in the declaration of God's most cherished purpose as regards the children of men would not have found expression. No, the Spirit of God could put upon the lips of this the last and greatest of the prophets (see Luke 7:28) no other word than this: "Behold the Lamb of God, which taketh away the sin of the world" (John 1:29).

It was for *this* that the only-begotten of the Father had come. All else was secondary. He had come to redeem. True, as Israel's King He would exercise authority; as a Prophet He would teach and declare God's judgment; and as the Son of God He would work mighty works of love in the healing of the sick; but all this would be eclipsed beyond measure. No! In the opening of our Lord's matchless ministry so beneficent for broken hearts and diseased, leprous bodies, so blessed for the oppressed groaning under Satan's heel, so wonderful for the poor, the blind, the lame, Jesus' great forerunner John the Baptist could not have heralded the appearing of the world's only Hope in any other terms save those of redemption. The cross is unveiled — "Behold the Lamb of God!"

The Lord is stepping forth from thirty years of obscurity to meet the multitudes with their aching hearts and undone lives racked with infirmities of a thousand kinds. There has been a mighty stir, for John the Baptist has preached as none of Israel's prophets had ever done. He saw sin in all its horrors and pointing a finger of condemnation and crying out to small and great he says: "O generation of vipers, who hath warned you to flee from the wrath to come?" But there was to come one after him, the latchet of whose shoes he was not worthy to unloose. Many had been baptized in Jordan confessing their sins. Great as John was, he could do no more than apply the awful lash of the law and cry, "Repent!"

However, the Son of God suddenly appears. There He stands in the midst of the multitudes. He, too, had asked for baptism, overwhelming the Baptist with a sense of unworthiness, not that He needed to repent or confess any sin, but that He might even now declare His oneness with sinful men and foretell in Jordan's waters, which signified death, what would hereafter take the form of an utter identification with the sin of the world on Calvary's cross. What could the Baptist say as he saw the Spirit of God descend upon Him like a dove? Only one thing, "Behold the Lamb of God, which taketh away the sin of the world."

He must speak in terms of the cross. None other could befit the Saviour. None other would tell the story. Any other would be to defraud the multitudes that surged about John, the preacher.

If there are those in our day who either are not willing to accept the implications of John's words, or perhaps are unable, we can be sure that it was not so with the throngs of John's day — rich and poor, ignorant and lettered, rulers and subjects. They understood. I am not saying that the glories of the cross were open to them. Redemption was not yet accomplished. What I am saying is that they were fully aware of the fact that John the Baptist was speaking of sacrifice. Were not the highways leading to Jerusalem even then filled with innocent lambs being driven to the temple for Levitical sacrifices of the accustomed Jewish worship? To the Jews, John's manner of heralding the long hoped-for Advent could have but one meaning.

John the Baptist, standing at the close of the Old Testament dispensation (he is the last of the prophets) and at the same time ushering in the New, speaks the Bible's most significant word, the word in which the Book finds its unity, and the world its hope of redemption. It comes at last as an answer to Isaac's anxious query, "Father, behold the fire and the wood, but where is the lamb for a burnt offering?" Jesus said that Abraham saw His day and rejoiced. This was the Day to which He referred, when seeing the Messianic Hope in the light of the Holy Spirit's inspiration, he confidently replied, "My son, God will provide himself a lamb for a burnt offering."

Let me repeat, here was at last God's sweet and lovely provision for the age-old longing of the heart. How it charges with meaning the Baptist's cry: "Behold the Lamb of God, which taketh away the sin of the world."

It is not a popular doctrine today. The Church, deceived by "the father of lies," is turning away from the cross, to her infinite shame and loss. She will never find victory in any other. The purpose of these studies is to bring her back to the cross.

Here is found, we cannot repeat it too often, the Bible's central message. The highways of Biblical truth converge on the cross. In that great book, *Blood Covenant*, Dr. Trumbull points out in a study which took him to the altars of peoples the world over, that the tribes of all the great human family without exception practiced blood sacrifices in their worship. He wisely states that far from discrediting the Biblical concept of blood atonement in view of the primitive state of such peoples, it rather proves that the instinct of the race (though perhaps crudely and erroneously expressed) runs parallel with Revelation in which the perfect Sacrifice is provided.

Praises forevermore as with gratitude that can never be measured we behold the Lamb of God which taketh away the sin of the world!

19

DESTROY THIS TEMPLE

THERE IS A WORK of art which presents the boy Jesus with an armful of wood on His way to Joseph's carpenter shop. The rays of sunlight which fall across His shoulders leave the shadow of a cross upon the earth beside Him. It is, of course, nothing more than an artist's conception, and yet how true. For the cross was the Saviour's supreme objective. He did not stumble upon it, as when one, walking in the dark, stumbles over an unseen object. He had seen it from afar and strode forward to embrace it as by a divine *"must."*

Men are born, it has been said, to live, while Jesus came into the world that He might die. Let there be no mistake about this. We are told in the Apocalypse that the Lamb (the Son of God) was slain from the foundation of the world. When Simeon, upon the occasion of the presentation of the Babe to the Lord, took the Child in his arms and blessed God, he turned to Mary and said: "Behold, this child is set for the fall and rising again of many in Israel; and for a sign which shall be spoken against; (Yea, a sword shall pierce through thy own soul also,) that the thoughts of many hearts may be revealed" (Luke 2:34, 35). How the sword must have pierced Mary's heart as years later she stood at the foot of the cross with Mary Magdalene and with her sister, the wife of Cleopas.

Early in the days of the Saviour's public ministry, the cross loomed before Him. In the second chapter of John's gospel on the occasion of the cleansing of the temple when the hostility of the Jews first became apparent, we have Jesus saying: "Destroy this temple, and in three days I will raise it up" (John 2:19). And lest there be a doubt as to the meaning of His word (the

74

Jews, of course, did not understand), John, as was his custom, adds the commentary: "But he spake of the temple of his body" (John 2:21).

The Jews were forever demanding a sign which they thought would put an end to all doubts. But the Saviour's reply was that no sign would be given to this generation but the sign of Jonah the prophet. "For," said He, "as Jonas was three days and three nights in the whale's belly; so shall the Son of man be three days and three nights in the heart of the earth" (Matthew 12:39, 40).

However, chapter 2 of John's gospel gives us a yet earlier foreshadowing of the cross. It was at the wedding feast in Cana of Galilee, where Jesus performed His first miracle, turning water into wine. Jesus' reply to His mother's anxious word, "They have no wine," "Mine hour is not yet come," can have but one interpretation. It was with this word that He marked the stages of His progress on His way to the cross, until at last in the Upper Room He says: "Father, the hour is come: glorify thy Son."

The question, of course, naturally presents itself: But why does this lovely festive scene turn the Saviour's thoughts upon the cross that awaited Him? Why do the joys of a Galilean wedding bring the awful scenes of Calvary before Him? The answer is found if not in the immediate text, then surely in the context of the Scriptures as a whole. Marriage in the Scriptures is fraught with symbolic meaning. Paul could not write of marriage as he does in Ephesians 5 without coming to an abrupt halt and saying: "This is a great mystery: but I speak concerning Christ and the church" (Ephesians 5:32).

When John the Baptist was asked if he were the Christ, he said, "I am not the Christ, but that I am sent before him. He that hath the bride is the bridegroom: but the friend of the bridegroom, which standeth and heareth him, rejoiceth greatly because of the bridegroom's voice: this my joy therefore is fulfilled" (John 3:28, 29).

Jesus could not look upon the lovely bride and the proud groom of Cana of Galilee's nuptial feast without being strangely moved. Had He not come for a bride? Must He not go to the cross ere she be found? Adam's bride was taken from his very ribs. Where else would the Last Adam's bride be found? Ah yes, she would be taken from His wounded side. Lacordiare is quite right in saying that the Church was born crucified.

Surely all this throws light upon our Lord's first miracle. Wine? Why, of course. Wine must not be wanting at the feast, as it will not be wanting at the Marriage Supper of the Lamb. No symbol of the divine life, the life of the ages, eternal life, like wine. That is why it is still used in many churches in the Sacramental Supper. "This is my blood," said the Saviour, as He took the cup.

20

JESUS POINTS NICODEMUS TO THE CROSS

ONE OF THE FAVORITE Bible passages for
Christians in all lands is John 3, where we have the story of
Jesus' interview with the Pharisee, ruler of the Jews, named
Nicodemus. The Saviour brushes aside formalities and gives the
proud ruler to understand that all his strict religiosity would go
for nothing as regards entering the Kingdom of God, except he
be born again. Nicodemus gets it from the Saviour's lips that
there could be no getting around this divine "must."

It is with His accustomed "Verily, verily," with which important matters relative to eternal life were wont to be given
special emphasis, that the Saviour declares to Nicodemus that
he must be born again. Jesus speaks with the authority which
was His as the Son of God, affirming that without a rebirth
through the Spirit Nicodemus could not even see the Kingdom
much less enter in.

What seems to attract the attention of preachers and evan-
gelists above all else is the fact that the Holy Spirit, according
to our Lord's word to Nicodemus, is the divine agent who brings
about this overwhelming change which the Redeemer insists is
nothing short of being born again. It baffled Nicodemus, who
says to Jesus, "How can these things be?" It has baffled thousands upon thousands over the years. Goethe, the great Ger-
man poet, was once asked if he believed in this second birth of
which our Lord speaks. His answer was, "How can I doubt it
when the mystery of the first birth is so great?"

Jesus tries to help Nicodemus by means of a simple illustration. "The wind," he says, "bloweth where it listeth, and

thou hearest the sound thereof, but canst not tell whence it cometh, and whither it goeth: so is every one that is born of the Spirit" (John 3:8). It might be retorted (some of us are so very smart!?) that the movements of winds are no longer mysterious since science has shed so much light on the why of such atmospheric tides. Be that as it may, the fact remains that it is all invisible, and so is the working of the Holy Spirit. Furthermore, as regards those who have been born of the Spirit, you cannot say *why* they do this or that or why they are thus and so, inasmuch as the ordinary motives that actuate men in their natural state no longer obtain in these. They are moved by the winds of God and do very strange things as witnessed by the Livingstones, the Booths, the Allen Gardners, the Josephine Butlers, the William Careys, and the unnumbered host of others, peers of the Church.

But what is of supreme significance in view of our thesis, *The Cross Through the Scriptures,* is the fact that our Lord finally takes Nicodemus to the cross as He says, in effect, "This is what the Holy Spirit uses to bring about the second birth. Here is where it is effected." We shall see directly that though the Holy Spirit brings it about, yet He does not work on His own. It is in and through the Crucified.

Nicodemus persists in his ignorance. However, his obstinacy was done away with at last for it was he who assisted Joseph of Arimathea at the cross and at the tomb. "If I have told you earthly things, and ye believe not, how shall ye believe, if I tell you of heavenly things?" And now comes the sublime, the glorious word which has been our goal since we began this chapter. We tremble, our hearts are moved as nothing else could ever move them.

"And no man hath ascended up to heaven, but he that came down from heaven, even the Son of man which is in heaven.

"And as Moses lifted up the serpent in the wilderness, even so must the Son of man be lifted up: that whosoever believeth in him should not perish, but have eternal life" (John 3:13-15).

Whereupon comes the immortal John 3:16, the Bible in miniature. If the believer is unable to recite any other text from the Word, this one is remembered and cannot be forgotten. "For

God so loved the world, that he gave his only begotten Son, that whosoever believeth in him should not perish, but have everlasting life."

So our Lord links up the second birth with the cross. Nicodemus is taken to Calvary. But Calvary, you say, was not yet a fact. Much time would pass before the cross be lifted up and the Son of God be crucified in immeasurable ignominy and shame to die a felon's death between two thieves.

The answer is found in the fact that in a sense we must begin at the cross and read backward. For the life of Jesus our Lord finds its deepest meaning in the cross. Others might not know, *but He knew* that all else was only a preparation for *this*.

Ah yes, it is when the Holy Spirit unveils the cross that hearts harder than flint are broken, souls as impervious to the entreaties of God as granite rock to water, are pierced with conviction, and sinners as unlikely to repent as tigers of the jungle, are broken down in tearful confession.

You cannot look upon God (to look upon the Crucified Saviour is to see the glory of God) pierced by the Roman soldier's spear with blood and water gushing forth, blood for the remission of sins, water for renewal of life, and not experience infinite gratitude. Faith wells up as naturally as water in a fountain. Such a God cannot be resisted. You are born again, for the Spirit works through the cross even as the cross leads the Spirit.

21

FOLLOWING JESUS MEANS
BEARING HIS CROSS

THERE WAS NATURALLY a certain reserve in Jesus our Lord regarding that which awaited Him at the end of the road. His disciples would not be able to bear it. But the moment came when He felt He could speak freely and, as it were, hide nothing. It came when—in answer to the question, "Whom do men say that I am?"—Peter answered, "Thou art the Christ, the Son of the living God."

"From that time forth," so Matthew tells us, "began Jesus to shew unto his disciples, how that he must go unto Jerusalem, and suffer many things of the elders and chief priests and scribes, and be killed, and be raised again the third day" (Matthew 16: 21). The hour had come when the veil must be drawn aside, so that the disciples might see what lay ahead.

But the impulsive, self-asserting Peter was displeased. What in the world was Jesus thinking of? This was too much. This could not pass unchallenged. Peter felt that it was up to him to straighten the Master out in his thinking. "Peter," we read, "took him, and began to rebuke him, saying, Be it far from thee, Lord: this shall not be unto thee." And, of course, Peter was right from the human viewpoint.

How severe, however, was the Saviour's reply. "Get thee behind me, Satan: thou art an offence unto me: for thou savourest not the things that be of God, but those that be of men." It was Peter who needed to be straightened out. Yea, and all those to whom the cross is an offense.

The cross is still a stone of stumbling to the Jews, and foolishness to the Greeks, as Paul wrote to the Corinthians. Many of the followers of Christ prefer a theology hammered out on most any anvil, rather than that of Calvary. And oh, how many there are who, anxious for the favor of God, put the cross aside to trust rather in their own good works, or the elaborate ceremonies of the church, or some strict adherence to a system of doctrines. We just must admit that the cross will ever be utterly repugnant to all those who are resolved to glory in their own merits.

The occasion, for our Lord, must be put to good use, to drive home the greatest lesson of all with regard to the Christian life. It was then, Matthew tells us, that Jesus said to His disciples: "If any man will come after me, let him deny himself, and take up his cross, and follow me. For whosoever will save his life shall lose it: and whosoever will lose his life for my sake shall find it."

How the sinful nature of man shows up in all its heinous selfishness in the light of the great paradox of the Gospel supremely exemplified, as it is, in the cross of Christ! However, it is a Law written deep into the very constitution of the very universe. If I am unwilling to renounce "self" and take up the cross in a thorough-going identification with the Crucified-Risen Son of God, however great my imagined virtue, I am on the road that leads to death; I shall eventually lose all, however much I may seem to gain. On the other hand, if with Paul, I am willing to bear in my body the marks of the Lord and go forth from "self" in the service of others, I shall find that all is mine. For as Sadu Sundar Singh was wont to say, "The cross is Heaven."

"Christ died for all," as it is in Paul's second epistle to the Corinthians, "that they which live should not henceforth live unto themselves but unto Him which died for them, and rose again" (II Corinthians 5:15).

The cross not only assures us of the forgiveness of our sins and reconciliation with God, but declares that we too must die and be raised up in newness of life. It were better to say that, judicially, we *have* died, and *have* been raised up with Christ.

"For you have died and your life is hid with Christ in God" (Colossians 3:3).

The most emphatic expression of this fact in all the New Testament is found in Romans 6, where we are told that the old (unrenewed) self was nailed to the cross with Him (Christ) in order that (our) body (which is the instrument) of sin might be made ineffective, and inactive for evil, that we might no longer be slaves of sin (Romans 6:6, *The Amplified Bible*).

Whereupon we are commanded to reckon ourselves dead in relation to sin and alive unto God (Romans 6:11).

22

THE DISCIPLES FOLLOW JESUS, TREMBLING

THE LORD JESUS had spoken to His disciples about the cross, but the time had come to speak even more clearly. The veil is drawn aside more fully. Details heretofore not mentioned are added. It was a terrifying experience for the disciples. They were afraid.

It is Mark in the tenth chapter of his gospel who gives us a detailed account of what happened. "And they were," he writes, "in the way going up to Jerusalem; and Jesus went before them: and they were amazed; and as they followed, they were afraid. And he took again the twelve, and began to tell them what things should happen unto him" (Mark 10:32).

There was that in the Saviour's manner which spoke of crisis. He was setting His face like a flint, as the prophet said He would (Isaiah 50:7), to go to Jerusalem knowing full well all that awaited him. We do wrong in thinking that it was all a plan which was working itself out willy-nilly, as we say, a more or less inevitable procedure of a somewhat mechanical nature in which Jesus moves along in a fatalistic fashion with no other choice of His own possible. Were that true the glory and atoning efficacy of the cross would be wanting. No. He could have chosen an easier path. He could have by-passed Calvary. As a man, and He was a man in the truest, fullest sense (God manifested in the flesh, true, but still a man who could be tempted in all points like as we, yet without sin), as a man, I repeat, he had to make His decisions in the same way all men must make them. That is to say, in the exercise of His will. What it cost we will see later when we come to Gethsemane.

It was evidently a moment of tremendous decision. It reflected in Jesus' majestic manner, overwhelming in its awful import. It went through the band like a terrific shock. The disciples followed on afraid. "Behold," said the Master, "we go up to Jerusalem; and the Son of man shall be delivered unto the chief priests, and unto the scribes; and they shall condemn him to death, and shall deliver him to the Gentiles [it was from Caiaphas to Pontius Pilate that He went bound as a criminal to be judged]: and they shall mock him, and shall scourge him, and shall spit upon him, and shall kill him: and the third day he shall rise again" (Mark 10: 33, 34).

Ah yes, our Lord knew even to the last detail. Nothing was hid from Him, who from eternity had chosen to do His Father's will, for was not the Lamb slain from the foundation of the world? The choice was made ages upon ages before, but the Man Christ Jesus, as such must choose afresh with the grim facts before Him. It called for all the resolve of His holy soul. There was that in it which man in his puny self could never comprehend. To atone for the sins of the world, to bear the chastisement due to the crimes, and sins, and wickedness of all the years in the history of sinful men, to satisfy the claims of the divine government so shamefully flouted, to express God's love to the fullest for mankind gone astray, and at the same time His awful loathing for sin, God's holy, righteous wrath against all the wickedness of the children of men — who could ever grasp the meaning of such an achievement? Who would presume to know all that was in the cup which Jesus our Lord drank to the dregs?

But let us rather dwell for a moment on the victory, though, of course, we must not differentiate between the cross and the Resurrection in this way. It was all victory from start to finish, however great the shame and the ignominy, and the seeming defeat. These are two aspects of one great Fact. Mabie is right in speaking of "the death-resurrection-mid-process." The glory of the Resurrection was in the death, as the power and virtue of the death are in the Resurrection. No one who makes an honest examination of the evidences can fail to arrive at an absolute assurance as regards this, the Central Fact of History. Read Morrison's book entitled *Who Moved the Stone?*, and see how this modern Thomas, after an honest examination of the evidences, cried out as did his predecessor: "My Lord and my God!" The empty tomb is as clearly evidenced as Calvary's cross, for without the former, the ignominy of the latter could never have been offset. Without the Resurrection, the cross would never have been more than the greatest miscarriage of justice in all the history of the world, and instead of bringing the un-numbered millions of redeemed men and women to faith and redemption, it would only have led them to despair and the denial of all hope.

But let us return to our text, for there is more of vast sig-nificance in the context. Mark records how immediately there-upon, John and James, the sons of Zebedee, come to Jesus say-ing: "Master, we would that thou shouldest do for us whatso-ever we shall desire." The Master bids them make known their wish. "Grant unto us," is the amazing request, "that we may sit, one on thy right hand, and the other on thy left hand, in thy glory."

Now the occasion was blessed in that it gave Jesus the opportunity to drive home a tremendous lesson with regard to glory and the cross. "Ye know not what ye ask," is the answer. "Can ye drink of the cup that I drink of? and be baptized with the baptism that I am baptized with?" On another occasion our Lord spoke of how straitened He was until the baptism with which He was to be baptized should be accomplished (Luke 12: 50). So there is no doubt as to the meaning. It was His cross.

So here it is. We would all like to come to glory and sit at the Saviour's right hand in His Kingdom. The condition, how-ever, is the cross. Jesus Himself came into His fullest glory by way of the cross. "Father, the hour is come; glorify thy Son," was the Saviour's prayer as in the Upper Room He expressed His farewell message, and prayed His high priestly prayer, be-fore going to the cross.

Would you be glorified? Would you sit, even now, with the Risen Christ in heavenly places? You may, as may be seen from the import of Ephesians 2:4-6. But the condition is the same as the one put before John and James. It is the cross. See Gala-tians 2:20, the door through which Paul entered.

23

THE "I AM" OF JESUS
CONFIRMED BY THE CROSS

THE CONTROVERSY in the gospel according to John, between Jesus and the Jewish authorities as regards His claims to be the Messiah, the Christ of God, and which runs straight through John's gospel as a major key, comes to a grand climax in the eighth chapter where we have the Jews taking up stones to stone Jesus. He had dared to say: "Verily, verily, I say unto you, Before Abraham was, I am." This was too much.

There had been a growing discontent. Jesus had greatly offended the princes of Jewry in the cleansing of the temple, in healing the sick on the Sabbath, and in so severely condemning the Pharisees for their pride and hypocrisy, all of which, however, might have been tolerated. Their hatred might not have burst into the flames which enveloped our Lord at Calvary, had it not been for this blasphemous (blasphemous for the rulers of Israel) assumption. How dared this Jew, born in a stable, this ordinary carpenter, this unlettered companion of publicans and harlots whose education had not gone beyond grade school (speaking in terms of our day) take upon his lips the sacred name of Deity by which Israel's God made Himself known to His people?

Only Jehovah, Israel's God, the True God, the God of Abraham, Isaac, and Jacob, the One who appeared to Moses and wrought liberation for Abraham's seed, dared say: "I am." Was it not known by all that the Lord had said to Moses, "Thus shalt thou say unto the children of Israel, I AM hath sent me unto you?" (Exodus 3:14). Nothing more heinous had ever been done in all Israel's history. Away with this mad impostor. Stones, stones, stones.

What inconceivable blasphemy! Were it not so outlandish, so utterly preposterous, so awfully sacrilegious one might laugh it off as a madman's obsession, this that the Nazarene was saying: "If ye believe not that *I am* [the *he* is not in the original] ye shall die in your sins" (John 8:24). No death could be too shameful, too cruel for such a hoax, such a fraud.

In the midst of the controversy, Jesus makes this transcendental affirmation so relevant to our thesis. The Master, so to speak, lets them have it full blast. "When you have lifted up the Son of man [on the cross], you will realize (know, understand) that I am He [for Whom you look]; and that I do nothing from Myself — of My own accord, or on My own authority—but I say [exactly] what My Father has taught Me" (John 8:28, *The Amplified Bible*). Or as it is in the *King James Version*: "When ye have lifted up the Son of man, then shall ye know that I am." Again, the *he* is not in the original.

Here we have Jesus staking all (if I may be permitted so improper an expression) on His cross. For the present stones; however, Jesus knew that before long it would be a cross. Now the amazing fact is this: whereas the Jewish princes, the high priest and his henchmen, felt sure that such an ignominious form of execution, reserved for the lowest of criminals, and the form of execution reserved among Romans for slaves who had no rights, would be the end of all claims on the part of Jesus to Messiahship; our Lord, the Son of God and Son of man, was sure that the cross would for all the ages substantiate His claims. At the foot of the cross men would find absolute certitude in the matter of the "I am" of Jesus.

For the rulers of the Jews it sufficed to know (Deuteronomy 21:23) that one put to death, hanged on a tree, was accursed of God. Why, His body must be removed at once lest the very land be defiled. Could anything, therefore, more unthinkable be conceived than a Crucified Messiah?

But Jesus affirmed that His claims to Messiahship, that with the fullest possible right He could say, "Before Abraham was, I am," would find its uttermost verification once He was lifted up on the cross. "When ye have lifted up the Son of man, then shall ye know that I am." The Jewish rulers staked all not many days later on the cross. Jesus ascended it, as a throne to rule the ages. He was sure that the cross would not only forever substantiate His claims, but bring in the age, the infinitely glorious age of the New Creation, the Old having been terminated on the awful tree — a curse, to be sure.

My task now is a very simple one. I need say nothing. History has spoken. The Father has spoken, for as we read in Romans 1:4, He has declared Jesus Christ to be His Son with power, according to the spirit of holiness, by the resurrection from the dead. Pentecost abundantly verified Jesus' claims, for did He not say that He would send the Comforter, and that the Holy Spirit would glorify Him? For twenty centuries that blessed Spirit of God, the Holy Spirit has been receiving the things of Jesus and showing them to men (see John 16:14).

That is why unnumbered millions of souls, burdened beyond measure with a load of guilt, have not only found peace at the foot of the cross but Heaven besides, not to mention blessings untold in the here and now. That is why so many millions in this Christian era have found the converse of the Saviour's dictum ("If ye believe not that I am, ye shall die in your sins") so utterly true. They that have believed, the Crucified-Risen I Am, Christ the Lord, has set free from guilt and shame and has gloriously redeemed.

24

JESUS SPEAKS TO MOSES AND ELIJAH OF HIS DEATH

WE DO NOT ASSOCIATE the Transfiguration with the cross, but judging from a significant detail which Luke has preserved for us, the deepest import of the mount of Transfiguration is found in Mount Calvary. It is the cross which gives its real meaning to the overwhelming scene which took place on the "high mountain" to which Jesus led Peter, James, and John for the purpose of revealing to them His glory. As our Lord in majestic splendor spoke to Moses and Elijah who appeared to Him, the theme of their conversation was "his decease which he should accomplish at Jerusalem."

Indeed, nothing so wonderful in all the realms of the Kingdom of God was ever known. The three hundred million universes of which astronomers are wont to speak are utterly eclipsed by its glory. Nothing in all the ages of Eternity will ever even faintly rival its moral splendor. All heaven, it would appear, stands in breathless expectation. Moses and Elijah come to the holy Son of God and commune with Him on the Mount of Transfiguration regarding His great work of redemption soon to be accomplished in Jerusalem.

The word in the original really means departure. "By faith Joseph, when his end was nigh, made mention of the 'departure' of the children of Israel" (Hebrews 11:22). It is the same word translated "decease" in Luke 9:31. Or it might be translated "exodus." Moses and Elijah spoke with our Lord of His exodus shortly to be accomplished.

It was a moment of Kingly glory when the Lord Christ

was transfigured. The disciples fell on their faces. They could
not bear such glory. John would remember when in later years
on the Isle of Patmos he fell as one dead at the feet of the Risen
Saviour who bade him not to fear. "They kept it close," Luke
tells us, "and told no man in those days any of those things which
they had seen" (Luke 9:36).

We read that Peter said unto Jesus, "Master, it is good for
us to be here: and let us make three tabernacles; one for thee,
and one for Moses, and one for Elijah: not knowing what he
said." Whereupon a cloud overshadowed them: and they feared
as they entered into the cloud. It was then that there came a
voice out of the cloud saying, "This is my beloved Son: hear
him." Matthew tells us that as the disciples "lifted up their
eyes, they saw no man, save Jesus only."

All of which, of course, is of vast significance for Christians
all down the ages. But it is when we face up to the fact that
there on the Mount our Transfigured Lord, His face shining as
the sun, and His raiment white as the light, spoke with Moses
and Elijah of His exodus to be accomplished in Jerusalem, that
we are left breathless with awe and wonderment. Indeed, not
simply *suffer*, but *"accomplish."* For the cross was achievement;
the cross was victory; the cross was the consummation.

What passed between the Saviour and these Old Testament
saints we can never know save that they spoke of that which
we can be sure had the hosts of Heaven leaning over their ram-
parts in breathless awe and expectancy. I say we will never
know and yet we *do* know, for the things consummated on Calvary's Mount are all in the Word.

These are all open secrets to believing hearts enamored of
the Christ. Moses had written of these things. David had heralded this hour. Isaiah, enraptured, saw these things and as no
other prophet of old declared the awful meaning of the stripes by
which we should be healed. The entire Old Testament with its
glorious Messianic Hope ever unfolding, derives its deepest, truest
meaning from this awful "exodus" accomplished at Jerusalem.

What passed between Jesus and Moses and Elijah as they
spoke of what should shortly be accomplished at Jerusalem?
What else could have passed if not the things which Jesus showed
His disciples as He appeared to them after His Resurrection,

opening their minds that they might understand what was written of Him in the Law, and the Psalms, and the Prophets? Must
not Christ suffer and enter into His glory so that repentance and
the remission of sins might be preached in His name among all
nations?

It may be difficult for us moderns and especially high-browed
theologians to accept "atonement through the blood." Many of
us seem to balk (it is such an offense to our pride), unwilling
to accept the redemption offered to all who will humble themselves at the foot of the cross and receive the unspeakable gift.
But these things heralded by the prophets and accomplished by
the Saviour—talked over on the Mount of Transfiguration with
Moses and Elijah—are still and forever will be the supreme de-
light of the unnumbered millions about God's Throne whose
hymns of praise center in the cross, and who commemorate the
exodus accomplished at Jerusalem. "Worthy art thou, O Lamb
of God," they sing, "for thou wast slain and hast redeemed us
to God by thy blood from every tribe and tongue and people
and nation." "These are they who have washed their garments
and made them white in the blood of the Lamb" (Revelation
7:14).

25

JESUS WILLINGLY OFFERS HIMSELF

IN THE TENTH CHAPTER of John's gospel we
have the Saviour speaking to the Jews regarding His great work
of redemption in terms best fitted to their racial temperament.
The Hebrew people were from their earliest origins shepherds.
"I am the good shepherd," says the Master, "the good shepherd
giveth his life for the sheep" (John 10:11).

It is with the authority which ever characterized our Lord
that we hear Him say: "Verily, verily, I say unto you, I am
the door of the sheep. All that ever came before me are thieves
and robbers: but the sheep did not hear them. I am the door:
by me if any man enter in, he shall be saved, and shall go in and
out, and find pasture. . . . I am the good shepherd, and know
my sheep, and am known of mine. As the Father knoweth me,
even so know I the Father: and I lay down my life for the
sheep" (John 10:7-9, 14, 15).

The sheep, our Lord declares, hear His voice and follow
Him, and to them He gives eternal life; they shall never perish,
for no one shall be able to pluck them out of His hand. "My
Father, which gave them me," Jesus goes on to say, "is greater
than all; and no man is able to pluck them out of my Father's
hand. I and my Father are one." But this infuriated the Jews,
who took up stones to stone Him. "Many good works have I
shewed you from my Father; for which of those works do ye
stone me?" It is the same controversy which led to the stoning
of chapter 8; for the answer of the Jews was, "For a good work
we stone thee not; but for blasphemy; and because that thou,
being a man, makest thyself God."

There could be no mistake about the implications of Jesus' words. It is the voice of the One who had dared to say: "Before Abraham was, I am." And so fuel is being added to the flame which would soon reach the proportions manifested at Golgotha. But there can be no toning down; Jesus the Lord who is the truth must speak the truth as regards His Person.

To what majestic heights do we have Him coming as here in John's gospel He affirms with immeasurable assurance: "And other sheep I have, which are not of this fold: them also I must bring, and they shall hear my voice; and there shall be one fold, and one shepherd" (John 10:16). Ah, but not without the cross. This is the door by which the sheep must enter.

Oh, hear the Good Shepherd as once more He points to the cross as the sublime goal of all His endeavor. "Therefore doth my Father love me, because I lay down my life, that I might take it again. No man taketh it from me, but I lay it down of myself. I have power to lay it down, and I have power to take it again. This commandment have I received of my Father" (John 10: 17, 18).

Let that be as it may. The Father and the Son are one. It is not our incumbency to attempt to unravel such mysteries as the Trinity involve. Thank God, we do not *have* to understand. We can believe and that is sufficient. Nothing more reasonable, more judicious, more commendable than to believe in such a One as Christ Jesus the Lord. As Dostoevski once said, "Even if Jesus were not in the Truth, I would still love and follow Him."

What I am getting at is that here we have the Voice of Ultimate Authority. There is no higher. "All things were made by him; and without him was not anything made that was made" (John 1:3). It is in the light of this that we must interpret the word which so infuriated the Jewish princes. "No man taketh it [my life] from me, but I lay it down of myself. I have power to lay it down, and I have power to take it again." Could anything more majestic be conceived?

We speak of the Divine Victim of the cross, the Lamb slain from the foundation of the world. But symbols are of value only up to a certain point. The lambs sacrificed by the Jewish priests in the temple knew not what should befall them. They went blindly to the slaughter. There was no choice made, nor any understanding involved. Not so, the Son of God. Ah me, what am I saying? Was there ever such insight and such understanding as our Lord's?

Now we must out with it. He chose! He willingly embraced the cross. He set His face like flint to go to Jerusalem. It was not the high priest, nor Pontius Pilate, nor Judas, nor the rabble, nor the Pharisees, nor the soldiers, nor Satan, nor any other entity, though, of course, it was all this. Let Peter say it as on Pentecost: *"Him, being delivered by the determinate counsel and foreknowledge of God,* ye have taken and by wicked hands have crucified and slain: whom God hath raised up, having loosed the pains of death . . ."* (Acts 2:23, 24).

Now it is this which gives to the cross its redeeming power before God and man. The blood of a "victim" would have had no redeeming virtue. Had the Saviour been taken to the cross by force, we would still be in our sins. True He fell beneath the weight of the cross, but every step the Master took along the stony way, the "Via Dolorosa," was a willing step. Our great Hight Priest mounts the altar and is Himself the Sacrifice. "So Christ was once offered to bear the sins of many; and unto them that look for him shall he appear the second time without sin unto salvation" (Hebrews 9:28).

26

THE CORN OF WHEAT FALLS
INTO THE GROUND

THE VISIT OF THE GREEKS recorded in the twelfth chapter of John's gospel opens a window through which we may peer for a deeper insight into the thoughts and purposes of Jesus our Lord. "Sir," they say as they address Philip, "we would see Jesus." For some reason Philip goes first to Andrew, whereupon the two inform Jesus of the request of the Greeks.

The Saviour's reaction, at least from the purely human viewpoint, is strange and altogether impossible to understand, except as we view it from the cross. There was every reason under the sun, as we say, for Jesus to rejoice over this fact. Here was good news. His own were increasingly hostile. His life was daily being threatened. Murder was abroad. Stones were being cast from all directions. The swelling tide of hate was threatening to break over all the dikes of restraint. How good to know that there were those who sympathized, and *they* representatives of the great Greek culture.

But instead of being pleased, or finding any ground for satisfaction, our Lord utters a cry of pain. His heart is wrung. Grief wells up in His soul. "Father," He exclaims, "save me from this hour," only to add, "but for this cause came I unto this hour" (John 12:27).

So strange is Jesus' behavior that we might not be able to grasp the meaning of it all were it not that the Lord Himself opens it all up to us and gives us the key, as it were. We see from His words that the request of the Greeks suddenly focused the Master's attention upon the cross. What was ever in the deepest depths of His soul, namely, that He was to be the fulfillment of the Passover Lamb's implication, a sacrifice to put away the sin of the world, comes rushing to the surface. He had a baptism to be baptized with and how He was straitened until it should be accomplished.

But we must let Him speak: "The hour is come, that the Son of man should be glorified. Verily, verily, I say unto you, except a corn of wheat fall into the ground and die, it abideth alone: but if it die, it bringeth forth much fruit. He that loveth his life shall lose it; and he that hateth his life in this world shall keep it unto life eternal. If any man serve me, let him follow me; and where I am, there shall also my servant be: if any man serve me, him will my Father honour" (John 12:23-26).

And then lest there be any doubt as to the meaning of His words, Jesus draws the veil aside yet more. "Father, glorify thy name." We read that a voice from Heaven then came, saying, "I have both glorified it, and will glorify it again." The people said that it thundered; others said an angel had spoken. Ah, but the real thunder was the awful word which followed: "Now is the judgment of this world: now shall the prince of this world be cast out. And I, if I be lifted up from the earth, will draw all men unto me." "This said he," John adds, interpreting events as was his custom, "signifying what death he should die" (John 12:31-33).

So there we have it. We have the apostle's authoritative affirmation that the request of the Greeks had brought the cross sharply before our Lord's mind's eye. But why? It might humanly have been as a sweet melody; or as a flash of light in the midst of a storm at night to show the way. Yes, but Jesus is governed by a great supernatural purpose which embraces all the world and all the ages. Indeed, He is the great Atlas carrying the world upon His shoulders. And how are not only these Greeks but every tribe, and tongue, and people, and nation (as it is in the Apocalypse where we are told that millions from every kindred, and tongue, and people, and nation are gathered about the Throne of God singing a new song, and saying, "Worthy art thou, O Lamb of God, for thou wast slain and hast redeemed us to God by thy blood"), how are not only these Greeks but all mankind to see Jesus in His truest light as the Saviour of the world, except He first be lifted up? For Jesus Christ is essentially and forever will be the Crucified-Risen Lord. No one better than Jesus Himself could know that only at the foot of the cross would the children of men find their deepest souls' need met.

Ah yes, the Saviour might well have trembled and cried out, "Father, save me from this hour." The sweat of blood has not yet taken place, but the Son of God (may I repeat it?) has a baptism to be baptized with, and how He is straitened until it be accomplished.

The prince of this world holding sway over the children of men must be cast out; his authority must be shattered, his rights annulled; but this could only be done on legal grounds. The "accuser of the brethren" must be silenced. How awful to think that day and night he accused them before God (see Revelation 12:10), pointing to a broken law. How could they be redeemed — they were his? The devil must be silenced. His hold on the souls of men broken. But how was this to be accomplished? Only by the blotting out of sin and guilt (guilt which gave the evil one moral ground which God must respect) wrought through the shedding of the Redeemer's most precious blood on Calvary's cross. "And I, if I be lifted up . . . will draw all men unto me."

27

GETHSEMANE

WE HAVE COME NOW to Gethsemane's garden, where in a very real sense we have no right to enter. The disciples were not permitted to enter. The three who were chosen to accompany our Lord on the great occasions of His public ministry — Peter, James, and John — were not allowed to enter. They were brought closer but they were left behind, as we read in Luke's gospel, "about a stone's cast."

The truth of the matter is, we are not able to enter here. It is all wrapped in dark mystery. Many attempts have been made to decipher the mystery, but the darkness is as dense as ever. Of one thing we may be sure. It was not the ordinary fear of death in the common use of the term which can account for our Lord's agony. Of that we may be sure. Christians have gone to the stake singing. The martyrs of the Church have embraced death without a shadow of fear, rejoicing over the high privilege that was theirs. No, it was not the fear of death.

We read that Jesus left the Upper Room with His disciples singing a hymn. He knew that the hour had come. An opportunity had been given the traitor to repent; his feet had been washed even as the rest of the twelve. The parting words had been spoken, the high priestly prayer as we have it in John 17 had been offered. "Father," the Saviour had said, "the hour is come; glorify thy Son, that thy Son also may glorify thee." The brook Cedron had been crossed and the garden entered. The disciples had been requested to pray lest they should fall into temptation.

Whereupon Jesus, saying: "My soul is exceeding sorrowful, unto death: tarry ye here, and watch," withdraws into the dark shadows (for it was night) of the garden. "And he went forward a little," writes Mark, and fell on the ground, and prayed that, if it were possible, the hour might pass from him. And he said, "Abba, Father, all things are possible unto thee; take away this cup from me: nevertheless not what I will, but what thou wilt." We read that he came to the three but found them sleeping. Ah, the shame of it — Jesus with the burden of the world's sin upon Him, crushed by its awful horror, and the disciples asleep!

Three times He goes and three times He comes. He finds no comfort in His sleeping disciples. He must bear the anguish alone. Nay, an angel from Heaven comes to comfort. The Father could not spare His beloved Son, and sinful men, too. So the cup is not taken away. So great, Luke the beloved physician (strange that it should have been he) tells us, is our Lord's anguish that His sweat was as it were great drops of blood falling down to the ground.

In the epistle to the Hebrews, whose theme is the priesthood of Christ interceding for the people of God and making atonement for their sins, we are given the privilege of looking upon the scene which immortalized Gethsemane's garden. The veil is drawn just a bit. We are told that He who in the days of His flesh, when He had offered up prayers and supplications with strong crying and tears unto Him that was able to save Him from death, was heard in that He feared (Hebrews 5:7).

We need not try to grasp the meaning of it all. We can reverently, humbly turn to the Scriptures in their bearing upon the Saviour's wondrous work of redemption and find what they so graciously reveal to Faith. The theologian may have difficulty in fathoming the depths of Gethsemane. The sinner who has found peace at the foot of the cross understands. Love may enter where mere curiosity never will be able. You can never grasp the secret of another's suffering but by love.

The Saviour had warned His disciples saying that the prince of this world would come. It was the hour of the power of darkness. Satan entered into Judas. Peter would not accept the warning: the adversary sifted him as wheat. All hell was moving against the Son of God. The devil would find nothing in Him, but he would throw in all he had in an effort to do so.

Some of us may have had to face the foe, for we wrestle not with flesh and blood. But in dealing with the Son of man who had come to destroy his works (I John 3:15) the devil mobilizes the entire forces of his dark kingdom and brings them down upon this lonely Man. The oppression was such that He would have died of a broken heart before reaching the cross for the fulfillment of redemption's great work. Ah, the agony of that hour as with strong crying and tears the Son of God made supplication. An angel from Heaven comes to His aid. His cry is heard. He is delivered. He comes forth triumphant from Gethsemane, whose ground had drunk the sweat of blood.

Then, too, the symbolic language gives us the key. "Father, if it be possible, let this cup pass." Jesus only a few moments prior had spoken in these terms as in the Upper Room He took the cup and gave thanks and said, "Drink ye all of it; for this is my blood of the new testament, which is shed for many for the remission of sins" (Matthew 26:27, 28). Luke's word is even more graphic: "This cup is the new testament in my blood, which is shed for you" (Luke 22:20).

In other words, Gethsemane can only be understood in the light of Calvary. We dare not fragment so sublime a whole. It is all of one piece.

We might never have had revealed to us all the riches of grace (grace springing from the cross) but for Paul, God's chosen vessel. No one has ever looked so deeply into the wonders of Calvary's cross as the apostle to the Gentiles. It is he who dares to say that our Lord was made sin for us that we might be made the righteousness of God in Him. In the Galatian epistle he goes so far as to say that He was made a curse that we might be freed from the curse which the law pronounces. Here is where Gethsemane's awful mysteries are resolved. Ah yes, the Son of God might well recoil and in the agony of the sweat of blood cry out for the cup to pass, for in the cup was the sin of the world — the cup which He must drink to the dregs.

28

THIS IS MY BLOOD, SHED FOR MANY

THE SHEDDING of the Redeemer's precious blood began long before He was lifted up on the cruel cross. It began in the garden, as we have seen, when in the midst of anguish too deep for human hearts to grasp, the sweat fell from His brow in the form of great drops of blood. "My soul is sorrowful, even unto death," He had said to the disciples as He entered the shadows of Gethsemane. But it was not for any wrongdoing of His own. No sin had ever stained His wonderful life. He was the spotless Son of God.

As He comes forth triumphant from the garden to give Himself up to the armed mob — soldiers, rulers, priests, and all the rest — the traitor's kiss being the sign, the awful way of the cross now becomes stark reality. First, the midnight trials with all their mockery and sham and hate and deceit, and then Pilate.

The Roman governor was more noble than the Jewish princes. He saw that it was for envy, so Mark tells us, that the rulers of Jewry had brought this Man before him. He resolved not to give way to the rabble and availed himself of every artifice he could conceive to deliver Jesus from the criminal designs of priests and Pharisees, but all to no avail.

At last he is brought to his knees by the cry, "If thou let this man go, thou art not Caesar's friend: whosoever maketh himself a king speaketh against Caesar." They hated Caesar, but in that hour they made him their friend, that they might rid themselves of Jesus.

The blow is too much for Pilate. Above all else he must strengthen his tie with Caesar or lose his political head. Pilate washes his hands, but only increases the guilt of his soul. Jesus

101

is turned over to the Roman guard for their blasphemous bufoonery and then the nameless scourging. Oh, the cruel post, the awful Roman flagellation. The whip with its sharp cubical bones entered deep into the Lord's back, bared for the blows, and the post already black with the blood of its many victims, is splattered with the sacred blood of the Holy One by whom all things were made and in whose image man had been made. Victims were wont to die under the awful scourging. Jesus our Lord could not die save on the cross, but much blood was shed.

Whether the mock crowning of the King whom the soldiers were willing to take as such for their ribaldry and for the heightening of bufoonery and laughter, came before or after the scourging, is not of great moment. John says it came after (John 19:1). The fact remains that the soldiers in the midst of their mockery brought thorns which they gave the form of a crown and plaited the emblem of kingship upon the Saviour's brow; and so again the blood flowed freely. Little did the soldiers realize that nothing could have been more fitting. Jesus had refused an earthly crown, but He who bore in His body the sins of the world to put them away forever could not refuse this crown; for thorns are the symbol of sin.

Ah, the long road to Calvary, how stained with blood as the heavy word bore down upon the Lord's back, so bruised and bloody from the cruel thongs of the scourging. Little wonder that He fell after such blows and bleeding.

We have come to the place of a skull. The baptism with which Jesus said He was to be baptized and which left Him so straitened in the days of His public ministry, now straitens Him indeed. The soldiers do a thorough job (dare I put it that way?) and the sacred form is left nailed to an accursed cross between two criminals. It is not for me to enter upon a detailed account of the six hours of shame and torture and agony. The seven words (never were there such words) are well known. I am thinking of the blood. How it trickled through the long vigil which must have seemed like an endless eternity; for time as we know is a relative thing that can be enhanced immeasurably by pain.

Ah, but the great cry of victory comes at last. Little wonder that the rocks were broken, the graves were opened, the veil of the temple was rent, and that there was an earthquake as the Saviour cried out, saying, "It is finished." The graves of men's pride have been opening ever since; the rocks of their wickedness are still being shattered; the veil of the temple separating men from the Holy of holies has been rent asunder forevermore; and the earthquakes effected by the cross in the transformation of nations and tribes and peoples and tongues still shakes the earth.

But we must fix our attention upon a detail which the beloved disciple, who was with Mary and the women at the foot of the cross, has preserved for us.

No, the soldiers must not break the legs of the central figure. This they might do for the two thieves. But not for Jesus. It had been foretold that not a bone should be broken. John speaks of this. Furthermore, there was no need. Jesus was already dead. Seeing His work completed, He could in Kingly fashion dismiss His spirit.

Now here is the detail. John, greatly moved as we see from the reading of the text, tells us that a soldier thrust his spear into the Saviour's breast and that out gushed blood and water. Knowing as we do that in such a death, the blood gathers in the peracardium, we can faithfully say that the last drop of our Lord's blood was poured forth upon the earth. Why? We shall see in the following chapters.

29

THE CROSS IN THE RESURRECTION

WE HAVE COME to the empty tomb. Morrison in his book, *Who Moved the Stone?*, points out how well guarded it was: soldiers, a great stone at the mouth of the sepulchre (a cave fresh-hewn out of rock), and finally the seal of the Roman Empire. Caesar was committed; no one shall enter, much less shall One come forth. But the Saviour of the world comes forth. How? There is but one answer. "The Lord is risen indeed, and hath appeared to Simon," said the apostles to the two who came hurrying from Emmaus. However, the stone was rolled away that the women might enter, not that the Lord might go forth. There was no need of this for the liberation of the Risen Christ.

Now a strange thing happens, altogether contrary to the order of events as they are wont to occur in the life of man. However, in Jesus our Lord all is natural and yet supernatural, for He is the God-Man. Should a great disgrace befall me, ignominy and shame beyond measure so that I should be an outcast from society and looked upon with horror, naturally, were it to come to pass that I should be restored to the good graces of men with honor and high office, I would want them to forget and never mention my disgrace. I would, of course, myself be careful never to refer to my former shame, a thing of the past best forgotten. My friends would never think of holding it up before me. However, with Jesus it is not so. The Risen Christ does not say to His disciples, "Please, let's forget it" (the cross). On the contrary, He says in effect, "Let's remember it forever and let's herald it in all the world and placard it before the eyes of men everywhere and forever."

We read in the gospels how that our Lord, appearing to His disciples, as He did for forty days with many infallible proofs (Acts 1:3), took them at once without a moment's delay, back to the cross. He showed them His hands and His side. He identified Himself (there are false Christs—see Matthew 24:23, 24) by means of His cross. He is the Crucified-Risen Lord. Thomas with his doubts is told to reach forth his hand to thrust it into the wounded side of his Lord.

But this is not all; to the disciples the Lord says: "Ought not Christ to have suffered these things, and to enter into his glory?" (Luke 24:26). There is no thought of hiding or forgetting the shame. It is rather to be the basis, the theme of the disciples' preaching, for Jesus says to them: "It behoved Christ to suffer, and to rise from the dead the third day: and that repentance and remission of sins should be preached in his name among all nations" (Luke 24:46, 47).

The Risen Lord goes so far as to say in effect that this (the cross) was what the Holy Scriptures all through the Old Testament were portraying and foretelling. He opens their understanding that they might understand the Scriptures, saying that what was written in the Law of Moses, in the Prophets, and in the Psalms regarding Him was now fulfilled.

In speaking to the two on the road to Emmaus, saying, "Ought not Christ to suffer," He takes them through the Bible, beginning at Moses, to show them how that these things concerning Him were all written centuries before His coming. These who for years had read the Old Testament and had heard it expounded by the Rabbis, see for the first time its deepest purpose and intent. They see their Risen Lord as the Crucified, placarded across the pages of Holy Writ. These "negatives" of the ancient writings of the prophets as they pictured what should befall the Messiah, now are seen as "revealed" at Calvary.

No, the Risen Christ does not ask His disciples to forget what took place at shameful, execrable, ignominious Golgotha. On the contrary, He bids them never to forget. How could they when the Sacramental Cup which showed forth His death until He should come again was to be the central token of their communion for all the ages? They were commanded to go forth and preach the Gospel to every creature, the Gospel which Paul the apostle to the Gentiles declares is essentially that Christ died for our sins and that He was buried and rose again the third day (I Corinthians 15:1-4).

Ah, but they were now seeing the cross in the light of the Resurrection. Who said, disgrace, ignominy, and shame? Why, now they were all seen to be simply because the Lord Christ in infinite condescension and love was willing to be made sin that those who received Him as Saviour might be made the righteousness of God in Him. It was my curse He bore, so with Paul I will say: "God forbid that I should glory, save in the cross of our Lord Jesus Christ, by whom the world is crucified unto me, and I unto the world" (Galatians 6:14).

Never was there such a victory. The head of that old serpent the devil was bruised. The rights and authority of man's greatest enemy were forever annulled. Through death the Redeemer destroyed him who had the power of death, that is to say, the devil (Hebrews 2:14). If the Son set you free, ye shall be free indeed. Only in the eternal ages to come will there be time (if in eternity there can be time) to sufficiently praise such a Saviour — infinitely adorable as is He.

Part Three

THE CROSS
IN THE
EPISTLES

30

PAUL DISCOVERS THE CROSS

No ONE HAS EVER gloried in the cross of Christ as did Paul, the apostle to the Gentiles. Others have gloried in the cross; but Paul's cry was: "God forbid that I should glory, save in the cross of our Lord Jesus Christ" (Galatians 6:14). It was the alpha and the omega of the apostle's life, the dynamic of his missionary labors, the very heart of his epistles, and the soul of his preaching. Nothing else could rival its matchless glory even for a moment. Our concern now is, how did he arrive at such a devotion, the supreme passion of his life?

The question takes us to the book of the Acts of the Apostles, the ninth chapter, where we have the story of his conversion. This one who as a Christian said that he counted all else but dung that he might win Christ, was just as vehement in the days of his unbelief when as a Jew and a Pharisee he persecuted the Church, determining by whatever means to uproot and destroy this fast-growing tree which threatened to spread over the earth. It was his duty to hale Christians to prison, to make them blaspheme the Holy Name by which they were called, and if necessary to see to their being stoned, as in the case of Stephen, the Church's first martyr.

It is all down in black and white, as we say, on the pages of Holy Writ. It seems that Saul of Tarsus, as he was then called, was a veritable tiger, for we read that he breathed out threatenings and slaughter against the disciples of the Lord Jesus Christ (Acts 9:1).

But on the road to Damascus as he galloped proudly toward that great city in order to undertake there, too, the imprisonment

109

of Christians and the destruction of the sect, one of the greatest of the events of history took place. This we may safely say, for Paul is the foremost maker of history, outstripped only by the One with whom comparisons cannot be made. Saul meets Jesus. The risen Christ appears to him and he falls to earth, smitten with blindness by a glory which he cannot bear. "Saul, Saul, why persecutest thou me?" To which Saul answers, "Who art thou, Lord?" "I am Jesus," is the reply from the risen Christ, "whom thou persecutest: it is hard for thee to kick against the pricks." Saul, trembling with astonishment, takes at once the attitude which characterized him the rest of his eventful Christian life, namely, that of a soldier, and says: "Lord, what wilt thou have me to do?" Paul (now it is Paul) comes to attention and asks for orders.

Now the prime interest for us at this point is the fact that the Lord says to this enraged persecutor, "I am Jesus." Seemingly such a reply to Paul's question was clearly out of order. The answer should have been, "I am Christ," for this is the name becoming our Saviour as Paul then beheld Him. He is the Christ of God. As to His divine nature, He is the Christ; as to His human nature, He is Jesus. Paul is blinded by a glory he cannot look upon; it is all divine; the splendor is that of God. Yet the voice emanating therefrom is that of a Man. "I am Jesus." How very strange.

But no, it is all exactly right. Had the Lord said, "I am Christ," the effect would not have been the same. Saul (let us put it this way) might have gone on in his infernal way persecuting Christians and destroying the Church. For this man believed in the Christ, as all true Jews did. This was not the flaming point of controversy. "I know that Messiah cometh, which is called Christ: when he is come, he will tell us all things," said the Samaritan woman to Jesus. Saul would have said the same. What Saul did not believe was that Jesus, rejected and crucified as a blasphemous impostor, was the Christ. In that awful instant, the marks of which would be in his very body even until death, Saul *knew*. Never again did he harbor a doubt. He could more easily have doubted his own existence.

In that instant, one might say, Paul's (now it is Paul) theology was forged. The glory which had left him in the dust, blinded by a light which he was wont to say afterward was above the light of the sun, was none other than the glory of God. And yet the voice which from this unspeakable glory proceeded was the voice of Jesus. So for Paul, Jesus was the Christ, the theme of his early preaching. And Jesus Christ was God manifest in the flesh. In Him dwelt all the fullness of the Godhead bodily. All things both in heaven and upon earth were made not only by Him but for Him (see Colossians 1:16). Here we have the great apostle's Christology. The most emphatic declarations in all the Scriptures regarding the deity of Jesus Christ, our Saviour and Lord, are found in the epistles of Paul.

But we must hasten to our goal. How then did Paul come to forge a cross-centered theology? How did he ever arrive at the position expressed in his Galatian epistle where he declares that he will glory in nothing but the cross of the Lord Jesus Christ, saying that there, he, too, had been crucified unto the world and the world unto him? To find the answer we will have to follow him to the Arabian desert to which he betook himself after the never-to-be-forgotten experience of the Damascus road (see Galatians 1:17).

Paul desperately needed quiet for meditation and prayer. His world had been annihilated. Moses and the law were gone. Phariseeism was dead. Gamaliel was forgotten. The ancient ordinances had been eclipsed. He was no longer a Jew — he was a Christian. Christ filled his soul's horizon as the sun the day. Paul must forge a new world with Jesus Christ as center.

But this was not all. Paul withdraws to the Arabian desert with a burden that would have crushed, an agony that might well have taken him to his grave. It was the cross. How reconcile the glory of the vision on the road to Damascus with Golgotha's shame? Paul knew his Bible. How that awful word in Deuteronomy about the hanged one being accursed of God (he quoted it later writing to the Galatians) must have pierced his innermost soul. Could such ignominy and shame ever be brought into harmony with such glory and majesty as was the Christ's? Or must it forever be the terrible stumbling block that it was to Jews? Would the offense of the cross which to the Greeks was foolishness, never cease?

But Paul did not go to Arabia alone. Jesus his new-found

Lord went with him. There they communed as friend with friend. Paul tells us in his epistle to the Galatians that there in the desert lands of Arabia Christ the Lord was not only revealed *to* him but *in* him.

He tells us that he received his Gospel straight from Jesus Christ without any human intervention. And knowing as we do the outcome of it all as found in the apostle's epistles, we can, with perfect certitude, affirm that as he communed with his Lord, it was revealed to him that, though wicked hands had slain Him, yet it was in the determinate counsel and foreknowledge of God. Paul comes to see at last that it was the fulfillment of the ancient prophetic word, namely, that the promised Redeemer would be wounded for our iniquities, that the chastisement of our peace would be upon Him. Oh, what joy, when it began to dawn upon Paul that the sinner's justification was consummated in the Saviour's blood shed on Calvary's cross. He comes forth from his three years' retreat aglow with the message he would proclaim to all the world, namely, that while we were yet sinners Christ died for the ungodly. It was through grace that the Crucified-Risen Lord had met Saul the sinner. This grace was for all the world.

31

THE CROSS — FOUNTAIN OF FORGIVENESS

WE SHALL NOW follow Paul, the foremost of the apostles, chosen by the Risen Christ Himself to bear His name before kings, as he draws from the cross, inexhaustible fountain of blessings, the treasures of grace which he so lavished upon souls with immeasurable bounty. It is all in his epistles. We must listen carefully, for this man under the Church's head, the Lord Jesus Christ, is her master-builder, forging her doctrines, extending her borders as no other has ever done, and establishing the principles which should govern her to the end of time. True, he walked not with the twelve, nevertheless, even though his apostleship was contested by many in his day, none was ever so worthy of it, or so completely authorized by life and deed and achievement to be called an apostle, as Paul.

What does he say as to the cross of Christ in which alone he would glory? Let us begin at the beginning. The beginning is God's forgiveness, for until a man's sin is forgiven, there is no hope. He bears the burden of his sins, and having violated God's holy law times without number, comes under His righteous judgment with no means whatever of justification. He slinks away in shame to hide, as did Adam and Eve from the face of God, forever. Were there no other hell, this were sufficient.

But, the apostle tells us, Christ died for our sins. Furthermore, this, he says, is the Gospel (I Corinthians 15:1-3). All the rest is but fruits of the tree, or if you prefer, happy circumstances accompanying the central fact.

Of course, in a sense, Paul is not telling us anything. The

Saviour said it in the Upper Room. "This cup is my blood, shed for the remission of sins." But it needed to be reaffirmed, and that by one who himself by virtue of the fact had stepped from the ground of deepest enmity to highest favor, at a blow. No mitigating circumstances, no merits of any kind (out to destroy Christians and the Church, therefore stabbing at Christ Himself), no sign of a change of heart, just sheer hate of the deepest dye, but forgiven. Another had borne his guilt — the One he hated. Paul, no doubt, saw it a thousand times there in the Arabian desert alone with his Lord who patiently unveiled to him, even as He did for the twelve (eleven) after His Resurrection, the mystery of the cross.

Let us just face up to it as we have it in the Colossian epistle: "Giving thanks unto the Father, which hath made us meet to be partakers of the inheritance of the saints in light: who hath delivered us from the power of darkness, and hath translated us into the kingdom of his dear Son: in whom we have redemption through his blood [which, of course, is to say His cross), *even the forgiveness of sins*" (Colossians 1:12-14). In the epistle to the Ephesians it reads: "In whom we have redemption through his blood, the forgiveness of sins, according to the riches of his grace" (Ephesians 1:7).

In what sublime, what majestic fashion it is stated in the epistle to the Hebrews, whose major theme is this very fact (assuming that Paul wrote it; we do not know who the author was; the Church has ever assumed that it was Paul): "Who (Christ) being the brightness of his glory (the Father's), and the express image of his person, and upholding all things by the word of his power, when he had by himself purged our sins, sat down on the right hand of the Majesty on high" (Hebrews 1:3).

I seem to hear voices crying, "Away with this slaughter-house religion. We will have none of it. God is love — He needs no blood of a Redeemer's cross in order to forgive." An echo, it seems to me, of the cry: "Come down from the cross, and we will believe." Now the Church's position has ever been (I am proud to stand with her) that men believe and are saved because our Lord did not come down from the cross. A great Christian once said, "The nails could not have kept Him there if Love had not bound Him."

A scoffer of our times was known to say: "Of course, God forgives; it's His business." But it takes no great insight to see that an easy, cheap, forgiveness is of no value even on a merely human plane. A father, whose business it is to forgive everything his children do, who establishes no government and who enforces no law, is not worthy of the name and will at last come to grief in a home which will lose all semblance of such to become a horror and a shame.

No! Let us not deceive ourselves, there can be no government, whether human or divine, there can be no divine order, whether in heaven or upon earth, without law. And law has no meaning if there is no punishment for those who break it. Now if the demands of the law are violated, and mocked, and trodden underfoot, without any application of the righteous rigor of said law (it should be called punishment), what becomes of government? It collapses and anarchy takes over. If we will not believe in the divine, a glance at the human is sufficient. There is no government in all the world which does not punish wrongdoers. Without prisons, there could be no society.

But God is Love. Indeed, yet with all His love which can never be measured, He could not pass over man's sin, as though it mattered not to a holy, righteous God, to whom sin is an abomination, and who has declared that it would be punished. "The soul that sinneth, it shall die." Should He thus lightly pass over sin He would cease to be good, cease to be God; heaven would be hell, and God's throne a joke.

Yes, it is God's business to forgive, for He does love the sinner though He hates his sin. That is why from the very dawn of history when man fell into sin a Redeemer was promised (the seed of a woman) who would undo the work of Satan and free the children of men from the devil's thralldom and sin's guilt. It was not to appease God's wrath that the Saviour died on Calvary's cross, but to give free reign to His love for the sinner, while at the same time His awful wrath against sin might be made manifest, and the righteous claims of a holy government fully satisfied. Without this, not only would the divine order collapse and God cease to be God, but even man made in the image of God would be an orphan forever bereft of a God worthy of his love and adoration.

No, let us not be deceived and embrace a false hope, but let us join the innumerable throng who about the Throne of God sing the new song — the song of the redeemed:

"Worthy art thou, O Lamb of God, for thou wast slain and hast redeemed us to God by thy blood . . . ."

32

DECLARED RIGHTEOUS BY VIRTUE OF THE CROSS

PAUL'S BOUNDLESS GLORYING in the cross, at least on the purely human side, springs from the fact that it meets absolutely every aspect of man's fallen state. ("All have sinned, and come short of the glory of God," Romans 3:23.) Man desperately needs to be forgiven, cleansed, restored to God's favor, in a word, redeemed. And lo, "there is a fountain filled with blood drawn from Emmanuel's veins, and sinners plunged beneath that flood lose all their guilty stains."

We seem to have forgotten and beaten a hasty retreat to the psychiatrist. And, of course, that is good as far as it goes. But the stain of sin remains, and guilt continues to burden the soul until faith hies away to Calvary where, though the crime be ever so great, and the shame ever so deep, and the sin ever so heinous, there is deliverance that will satisfy for both time and eternity, leaving nothing to be desired.

But we have only begun to tap the mine with its inexhaustible treasures of grace. We are not only forgiven as we embrace the Crucified-Risen Lord. In view of the cross, which was such an utter liquidation of sin's account, the believer is declared righteous. "Justified by faith, we have peace with God through our Lord Jesus Christ," as it is in Romans 5. The reformers gave it out in mighty clarion notes.

However, *The Amplified Bible* presents the fact in stronger terms, terms which seem a more exact rendering of the apostle's thought. The sinner who believes and receives Christ is declared

117

righteous, acquitted, and given a right standing before God (Romans 5:1). It leaves one gasping with amazement, with "joy unspeakable and full of glory," as one comes to realize that such was the work of redemption consummated on Calvary's cross that, by reason of its infinite efficacy, God can conscientiously declare righteous, free from all guilt, the one who by faith avails himself of the "unspeakable gift."

Let us look deeper into this marvelous fact which, could we but appraise its fullest meaning, would banish forever all our fears, and heal the wounds of our sin-stricken hearts. Paul expounds it all in his epistle to the Romans, where he puts the whole world under conviction of sin, Gentiles and Jews, declaring that there is not one righteous, no, not one in all the world (righteous according to God's standard). As Paul analyzes the man of his times and states the case of the sinner, one cannot but blush for shame; and yet he is simply "taking the lid off the garbage pail" (please pardon the expression), as it has stood at God's doorstep since the fall of man. If you have any doubts, take a good look at the cross, where we have not only the supreme revelation of God's love, but also of sin's awful heinousness, its awful hellishness (no other term fits). The cross is the sinner's answer to God's overtures of love. "Let us slay him, for this is the heir," as in the parable. The sinner's attitude toward God has been portrayed for all time at Calvary.

Paul goes on to face up to the problem of God's righteousness in view of man's devilish rebellion against the divine government. How pass over man's wickedness when there exists such a profound antagonism between the one and the other? Moses the great law-giver had declared that it was not possible for God to justify the ungodly, the wicked. Nothing more reasonable. Were He to do so He would cease to be just. The judge, who for bribes or other considerations, justifies the wrongdoer, ceases to be a judge, to descend to the level of the criminal he acquits. So with the Most High. Were He to declare free from guilt the sinner laden with shame in the defiance of God's law, He would stoop to the level of the wicked, and Himself become sinful. No, the Lord cannot justify the sinner.

Ah, but He found a way, a way so wonderful, so glorious, as to constitute itself the central glory of the Godhead. Nothing more blessed, more worthy of praise will ever be known throughout all eternity. Yes, He found a way whereby He could acquit the sinner who times unnumbered has trampled underfoot His law and mocked His government and defied His Kingship. It can never be impeached either by angel or devil. A flaw will never be found. No blemish, nay, never so much as a shadow of a stain, will ever appear. The Throne will forever be that of a Holy God whose righteousness will stand unsullied before unnumbered millions of angelic beings, and redeemed souls. The way is the way of the cross.

Man's sin *was dealt with.* Man's crimes were given their due. Man's rebellion and his wickedness were judged. "Now is the judgment of this world," said Jesus our Lord as He turned His face like flint toward the cross. It was a Man who bore the shame. It was no angel who died on Calvary. Nor was it God. It had to be a man — the God-Man. It was the sin of the world receiving its just due; else the Throne would not be free from the stain of unrighteousness. It was the world's sin being punished as the righteous claims of God's holy law demanded that it should be, else God's dealings with the sinner on the ground of mercy would be open to shameful impeachment.

Yes, God found a way to justify the sinner and yet remain just, as Paul puts it in Romans 3:26. Ah, wondrous work of grace which gives the believer such a standing before God that He may declare him righteous without the possibility of such a governmental procedure ever being challenged. Thus was "that old serpent the devil" who, we read in Revelation 12, accused "the brethren" day and night before the Throne of God, silenced, and man liberated from his awful thralldom. He can no longer point to a broken law. He has been silenced on righteous ground.

God declares the believer righteous, free from guilt, for he is in Christ who was made his sin, that he might be made the righteousness of God in Him (II Corinthians 5:21).

Is not such a One worthy of man's love and undying devotion? Do you wonder that Paul was determined to know nothing save Jesus Christ and Him crucified? If this does not make your heart sing, nothing ever will.

33

RECONCILED BY THE BLOOD OF THE CROSS

THE CROSS OF CHRIST is a circle of infinite dimensions that embraces all. There is no aspect of sin's dominion in the life of man which is not remedied by its divine potency. We shall see later how by it God brought order into the spiritual universe, chaotic because of the fall of Lucifer, Son of the Morning (Satan). No less is order brought into the vast realms of man's being, chaotic because of sin, by its immeasurable virtue.

Forgiven, as we have seen, declared righteous in view of the Sacrifice consummated by the Son of God — are we left to shift for ourselves as best we may with the terrible bent toward pride and self-will still mastering us? Are we only declared righteous without being made so? Such a work would not bring glory to God. Such a redemption would still leave man under the sway of the evil one with whom man's pride establishes an affinity.

Praise God, there is more in the cross of Christ for the believing heart, panting for a full-orbed deliverance. Let us turn to the Scriptures through which, as we are seeing, the cross runs as a flaming sun healing all with its beneficent rays. How tremendous the fact of man's reconciliation as we have it in Paul's epistle to the Colossians. Having spoken of the forgiveness of our sins through the Redeemer's most precious blood, the apostle goes on to say:

> For by him [Christ] were all things created, that are in heaven, and that are in earth, visible and invisible, whether they be thrones, or dominions, or principalities, or powers: all things were created by him and for him: and he is before all things,

and by him all things consist. And he is the head of the body, the church: who is the beginning, the firstborn from the dead; that in all things he might have the pre-eminence. For it pleased the Father that in him should all fulness dwell; and, having made peace through the blood of his cross, by him to reconcile all things unto himself; by him, I say, whether they be things in earth, or things in heaven. And you, that were sometimes alienated and enemies in your mind by wicked works, yet now hath he reconciled in the body of his flesh through death, to present you holy and unblameable and unreproveable in his sight (Colossians 1:16-22).

Indeed, it is the cross which is the ground of our reconciliation with the Father. Of what avail forgiveness, of what value justification, if the awful principle of enmity toward God is to go uncorrected? If the infernal sway of pride which alienates man from God is to receive no correction and he is to continue enthralled by the arrogance of the old nature which Paul tells us in Romans 8 is enmity toward God — if such is the case the forgiveness and justification emanating from the cross are not worth a pittance.

But no, such is not the cross of the Lord Jesus Christ in which the apostle so passionately gloried, refusing to glory in aught else, however great it might be. The ax was laid at the root of the tree as John the Baptist said it would be. If at the foot of the cross we are not reconciled to God, we have not seen its immeasurable glory, nor have we truly embraced the Crucified-Risen Lord who through death has reconciled us to the Father to present us holy and unblameable in His sight.

This fact shows up in the epistle to the Ephesians with even more captivating colors. The passage must be taken in all its breath-taking import: "He is our peace [Christ], who hath made both [Jew and Gentile] one, and hath broken down the middle wall of partition between us; having abolished in his flesh the enmity, even the law of commandments contained in ordinances; for to make in himself of twain one new man, so making peace; and that he might *reconcile* both unto God in one body by the cross, having slain the enmity thereby" (Ephesians 2:14-16).

Here we see that so potent, so all inclusive in its scope, was the cross of Christ, that not only was man reconciled to God thereby, but reconciled to all men (Jews and Gentiles, the wall

of separation broken down). If we do not come to the cross
with our racial discriminations, there is no hope. Law is impotent; but oh, the cross — I cannot stand there and hate my
fellow man whatever his color, for whom Christ died, as He did
for me.

"Having abolished in his flesh the enmity." "Having slain
the enmity thereby" (the cross). "He hath broken down the
middle wall of partition." Ah, these walls of separation between
man and God, as well as between man and man, the result, as
Paul says, being enmity. They were all annihilated at Calvary,
did we but have eyes to see, eyes illumined by the Holy Spirit.
May the Spirit of God give us grace to embrace the cross of
Christ in a new way that enmities whether between man and
God, or man and man may forever be slain.

The sister passage in Second Corinthians gives a yet clearer
focus; for here reconciliation is underscored as the very purpose
of Christ's coming. "God was in Christ, reconciling the world
unto himself." And to bring it to pass, He was willing for the
sin of the world to be imputed unto Himself, as it was at Calvary.
For He who knew no sin was made sin (Christ), that we might
be made the righteousness of God in Him (II Corinthians 5:19,
21). It leaves you breathless. Oh, this chapter five of Second
Corinthians, what amazing affirmations regarding the Redeemer
and His cross.

But let us not overlook verse 14, where we are told that inasmuch as Christ died for all, then judicially, all have died.
How else could this deep dyed principle of enmity which is in
our breasts, enmity toward God, enmity toward man, be dealt
with? Since my Saviour, as a Man judicially identified with it,
took it to the cross, how can I refuse to stand by faith with Him
in death so that I might be free?

There were two brothers in the flesh who had given place
to enmity for reasons we need not go into. They had not seen
each other for years. Hate had grown to infernal proportions.
It so happened that the father of these two died very suddenly.
They both came, of course, to their father's funeral. It so happened that these two, one coming in by one door, the other by
another, faced each other there before their father's coffin. It

was a heart-rending moment. They stood confused — and then in a surge of emotion they embraced each other. Enmity had died in their father's death.

And so our enmities, all of them, those toward God, those toward man, have died in our Saviour's death. We are reconciled through the blood of His cross. Are we willing to say "Amen," and enter in?

34

THE CROSS —
THE END OF THE OLD CREATION

WE HAVE COME TO Romans 6, which stands out as a veritable Everest in the midst of the high peaks of redemption. It has been called the Magna Carta of the Christian's liberty. The sinner has not only been justified (declared righteous, free from guilt, acquitted at the bar of divine justice) in view of the efficacy of the Redeemer's most precious blood shed for the remission of sins. He finds in the cross of Christ another boon no less essential to his well-being and happiness, namely, freedom from sin's inherent power to enslave and master him. Sin not only means guilt, it constitutes itself a tyrant who commands and is obeyed.

In Romans 5 the moral condition of the sinner is not taken into account. He may be the greatest of criminals on his way to the electric chair. But if he truly receives the Lord Jesus Christ as his Saviour, before God he is freed from guilt. He is justified, accounted righteous. The righteousness of Another, who was made his sin, is imputed to him.

The scene is a judicial one, even though some are shocked and rebel against such an interpretation. Yes, He is our Father, but also our Judge, without which He could not be our God. He cannot deal lightly with sin. It must be judged. If not in the sinner, then in Another, great enough and good enough to take the responsibility and to stand in the sinner's shoes and, having taken upon Himself the sinner's condemnation, to accept his punishment. There really is no other way.

Now all this Christ our Lord, in infinite condescension and love, did. "Being found in fashion as a man, he humbled himself, and became obedient unto death, even the death of the cross" (Philippians 2:8). This is something so great in the sight of God that on the ground of the righteous fulfillment of the demands of His law in the death of the One made sin, He can now conscientiously, as it were, declare the sinner who believes on Christ (made his sin on the cross) justified, that is to say free from guilt and in right relations with Himself.

But this is not the end. It is only the beginning. We should move immediately over into Romans 6. The divisions after all are artificial and do not exist in the original manuscripts. It is all of one piece.

Paul immediately raises the question of sin's power over man. "Shall we continue in sin that grace may abound?" (Romans 6:1). That is to say, is man to be justified in a legal sense, declared righteous, which seems to be the real implication of Romans 5, and yet left to the mercy of the ravages of sin as a devouring principle, a destructive, God-defying force in the life of one declared righteous legally, but still in actual fact unrighteous morally? It comes to this with many Christians justified but still essentially sinful. This in the history of the Church has been called "antinomianism." That is to say it matters not whether sin is still rampant in your life; what matters is that you believe and are consequently "justified by faith" and therefore have "peace with God."

But this does violence to the cross of Christ which is not only the ground of a right standing before God legally, having been freed from all guilt, but also the ground of a spiritual, perhaps better said, moral transformation in which the believer is freed from sin as a governing principle and the very righteousness of Christ made to operate in him. In other words, he is not only declared righteous, but made righteous.

Paul the apostle, moved by the Holy Spirit, puts it this way. And, of course, this is the way, the only way to take it. The possibility of the believer, justified in his Redeemer's blood, still living under the dominion of sin as a governing principle, stirs him to the depths. He cries, "God forbid." This to Paul is a caricature of the Gospel. "How shall we, that are dead to sin, live any longer therein?" Then comes the great declaration regarding the cross of Christ which makes Romans 6 the Everest that it is. "Our old man [the sinful self] was crucified together with him [Christ] that the body of sin might be destroyed, that henceforth we should not serve sin" (Romans 6:6). So we see that alongside the great word, "For the sinner Christ died," we must put the no less significant word, "With Christ the believer died." The Scriptures are most emphatic as regards this matter, which when left out of the picture impugns the righteousness of God and cuts in two the wondrous work of redemption consummated on the cross of Calvary by the Son of God. It was not only to put away the sinner's guilt and to give him right standing before God, but to break the backbone, as it were, of this monster called sin, and to set man free from his dominion.

We are to reckon ourselves dead to sin and alive unto God through Christ Jesus our Lord (Romans 6:11). As we do this we are assured that sin shall no longer have dominion over us (Romans 6:14). Here we have God's answer to the believer's sighs, and tears, and longings, and struggles, and prayers, and what not, in an ever repeated effort on the part of the believer to live a life of victory over "the world, the flesh, and the devil." Sadly, tragically, heart-rendingly, it all comes to naught. Self-effort cannot achieve what only Christ crucified could bring to pass. Here is God's answer. On Calvary's cross a cosmic blow was dealt to the monster. Sin as a governing principle in the life of man was taken down into death with Christ, Christ made sin in the economy of God. The old creation — life with its pride and bigotry and self-centeredness was ended when the Crucified cried: "It is finished." The curtain went down on history, as Watchman Nee is wont to say. It was the dawn of a New Age. In the power of His Resurrection the Son of God, Son of man, brought to light the "new man." If any man be in Christ, he is a *new* creation.

All this is as much a gift as forgiveness and justification. It springs from the same cross. We do not attain it by effort. We must rest upon an accomplished fact, namely, that Christ the Lord not only dealt with our sins on the accursed tree, but also with the sin, as a principle, that governs, in spite of all man's efforts to the contrary, his way and life. "Our old self *was*" (not *is*, as in the *King James Version* it is mistakenly rendered), I repeat, "*was* nailed to the cross with him" (Christ). It is an accomplished fact. Nothing can be added to it. Let us rest in all that Calvary signifies. Victory will be the result.

35

THE CROSS —
THE END OF LEGALISM

IT RUNS THROUGH Paul's epistles that the cross of Christ was the end of the economy of legalism. The law came by Moses, but grace and truth by Jesus Christ, so wrote John the apostle. But it took Paul, our Lord's chosen vessel to bear His name before kings, to fully expound this fact and to show how this came to pass.

In his epistle to the Colossians Paul says that the handwriting of ordinances which was contrary to us was blotted out, the Lord nailing it to His cross. Not only did He put away sin by the sacrifice of Himself, not only did He judicially put an end to the old creation, He terminated the old Jewish legal system which was so vitally related to both. Where sin has been cancelled, and the old Adamic nature has been annulled, the Saviour taking it with Himself to the cross, the legal system stemming from Moses no longer obtains. Its reason for existence has gone.

The Saviour Himself had paved the way for this even prior to Calvary. "Ye have heard that it was said by them of old time . . . But I say unto you." Now it is no longer, "Thou shalt not kill," but "Thou shalt love thine enemy."

The great classic regarding this matter is Romans 7. Here we are told that by means of the cross, our Lord and Saviour Jesus Christ took us out, in the most drastic fashion conceivable, from the old Mosaic system with its legal demands, its decrees, and its ordinances. It is declared with the authority God had given to the great apostle to the Gentiles, that Christians have died to the law by the body of Christ, that they might be married to another, even to him who is raised from the dead (Romans 7:4). Sometime ago the United States government issued a decree in which all soldiers whose names had been appearing (World War II) in the lists of those who had disappeared, were officially declared *dead*, regardless of circumstances, thus freeing thousands of semi-widows to remarry should they wish to do so.

The decree has gone forth from the very throne of God that Christians are to consider themselves dead to the law. The Lord Christ took that which was contrary to us and nailed it to His cross. We are free to marry another, even the Risen Christ. *This places us on ground so high that there need be no fear of wrongdoing because of freedom from a legal system.* Christ now is our life, and we feel as He felt and do as He did. John says we are to walk even as He walked (I John 2:6).

Paul takes his own experience to illustrate the matter. This shameful, heart-rending confession that follows in Romans 7 cannot be the voice of Saul of Tarsus, as some have thought, for Saul the Pharisee declared that as to the law he was blameless (Philippians 3:6). This sort of soul-searching, and agony, and inner conflict, was foreign to a Pharisee glorying in the law. No, it is Paul the Christian, but in a mistaken position. Here we have Paul under law, finding his utter moral bankruptcy apart from grace, and coming to the end of himself. Oh, that command: "Thou shalt not covet," how it scorched him, how it tormented him; for he finds, however much he may struggle, that it is not within his moral capacities to fulfill such an injunction. He would do good but finds he cannot, for evil is present; he is carnal, sold under sin. Yes, he delights in the law of God after the inward man; but he finds another law in his members, warring against the law of his mind and bringing him into captivity to the law of sin which is in his members. At last comes the cry of despair: "O wretched man that I am! who shall deliver me from the body of this death?" (Romans 7:24).

Anyone who doubts that this is the voice of Paul the Christian, let him put himself under the yoke of the law, forgetting for the time the redeeming grace of the Lord Jesus Christ, and see if he does not find himself in the same "slough of despond," and does not come to the same despair.

Then of what value the law? If the law awakens in me what it prohibits (see Romans 7:8, 9), is it good? Paul falls back in horror before such a conclusion. "The law is holy, and the commandment holy, and just, and good" (Romans 7:12). The trouble does not lie there. It is that when I would do good, evil is present with me. It happens that sin, that it might appear sin, works death in me, says Paul, by that which is good; that sin by the commandment might become exceeding sinful.

Here we have the crux of the whole matter; and to what a tremendous dictum it has brought us. The law is impotent (Romans 8:3). It only aggravates matters. It was never given to be kept, but to be broken. That sounds like diabolical heresy; but it happens to be pure Biblical truth. Read Romans 7, and see. "The carnal mind is enmity against God: *for it is not subject to the law of God, neither indeed can be*" (Romans 8:7).

Then why was the law given? It was given to show sin up for what it is. Some diseases have to be brought to a head; the physician must provoke a crisis before he can effect a cure. The law provokes the crisis, the cure is in the cross. The law was our schoolmaster, as Paul says elsewhere, to bring us to Christ, to crowd us to Christ, writes E. V. Maxwell in his book, *Crowded to Christ*.

Such a conclusion need not shock one. Augustine said it many years ago: "Love Jesus, and do as you please." Scandalous? No. For if you love Jesus, you will be united to Him; and that will mean a walk like His, and a love like His, and a life like His. We are "enlawed" to Christ (see I Corinthians 9:21). If you must have law, let it be this.

Coming back to Colossians where Paul says that the Saviour nailed to His cross that which was contrary to us, namely the handwriting of ordinances, the decrees of the old legal system, it is not surprising that in the very next breath he should declare that thus the Son of God spoiled principalities and powers, making a show of them openly, and triumphing over them in the cross. For Satan likes to drive us to Sinai that he may accuse, and lash, and oppress. The Holy Spirit takes us to Calvary. Here "the accuser of the brethren" was silenced. "And they overcame him by the blood of the Lamb, and by the word of their testimony; and they loved not their lives unto the death" (Revelation 12:11). Clearly only the cross avails in this awful conflict with the evil one.

36

THE CROSS —
IN THE HEART OF THE CHURCH

LACORDIARE, THE GREAT French preacher, was wont to say that the Church was born crucified. Indeed, it was even so. She was taken out of the wounded side of the Crucified, the last Adam, even as Eve was taken out of the first Adam's ribs. But the Church does not understand, which explains her spiritual impotence and lethargy. The world looks on and sees her divisions and rivalries and jealousies, and shakes its head, and is not convinced. Carnality, strife, rivalry, jealousy, and worldly ambition I understand, says the world, for that is the stuff I am made of. "We would see Jesus," said the Greeks to Philip. But Jesus did not accede to their wishes, as we saw in a former chapter. He said, No. First the cross (John 12:20-23).

And so it is with the Church. Men everywhere would see Jesus. But the Church can only show forth His glory by means of the cross. She must realize that she was born crucified, and that apart from the cross as we have it in Romans 6, she becomes impotent, overgrown with the weeds of pride and sectarian rivalries, not to mention other things yet more repugnant.

We have mentioned this in a former chapter. But it is too important for a mere passing reference. Ecumenicity is the fashion of the hour. It would not be possible for me to speak a contrary word to the great ecumenical movements of the Church in our times, for I have ever been all out for the unity of the Church and have given much of my life to promote a oneness among Christians, realizing that the Church is the body of Christ, that He is the Head, and that Christians are members one of another. If one member suffers, as Paul puts it, all suffer.

But ecumenicity can never bring about that oneness of believers for which Jesus prayed in the Upper Room. There is only one means in view of the inherent selfishness of men. There is but one remedy for that which even within the Church causes men to split up into rival groups. War, James tells us, does not spring primarily from economic questions, or commercial, or ideological, or national questions, but from the wickedness which he calls lust, in the hearts of men. The prophet knew what he was talking about when he said that the heart of man was desperately wicked and deceitful above all things (Jeremiah 17:9).

Indeed, there is but one hope. Pride, and rivalry, and denominational bigotry give way before one and only one potency. It is the cross. The Church must realize that she was born not Presbyterian, nor Methodist, nor Baptist, nor Congregational, nor Reformed, nor Anglican, nor any other thing. She was born crucified. Take the cross out of her heart, and the spirit of the world takes over. Christ is no longer the head; the subtle workings of "the flesh," ever latent as they are, take over and there is little of actual spirituality left.

The Ephesian epistle, Paul's great exposition of the origin, nature, unity, and warfare of the Church, is the never-to-be-surpassed classic. The age-old problem of the relations of Jews and Gentiles comes up. Never was there such a "wall of separation." The old Chinese wall cutting China off from the rest of the world was but a shadow in comparison. How unite Jew and Gentile? To the Jew the Gentile was a dog, a stranger to "the law." To the Gentile, the Jew was even more abhorrent. The antagonism humanly could never be removed.

The wall, Paul tells us, was broken down at the cross. "But now in Christ Jesus ye who sometimes were far off [Gentiles] are made nigh by the blood of Christ. For he is our peace, who hath made both [Gentiles and Jews] one, and hath broken down the middle wall of partition between us; having abolished in his flesh the enmity, even the law of commandments contained in ordinances; for to make in himself of twain one new man, so making peace."

The Lord had to take from the Jew his religion, as it were,

to bring him into oneness with the Gentile. Nothing separates people and locks them up in warring camps like "religion." The "contrary" thing as it is in the Colossian epistle, was nailed to the cross.

Here in Ephesians, Paul is as bold as a lion. He faces the two camps, Jews and Gentiles, and, as it were, bids them lay down their arms in view of the fact that both had been reconciled to God on the same ground, the ground of the cross, and that all enmity had been slain on the accursed tree of the Crucified-Risen Saviour. Could anything more wonderful be found, anything more vital, not to say revolutionary, both to the Church and to the world?

Paul is really saying in this, the sublimest and most majestic of all his epistles which has been called a veritable cathedral, that I (or you) may go on fomenting the pride of race, pride of group distinctions, not to say ecclesiastical, pride whatever its nature, but to do so is to violate Christ's masterpiece consummated on Calvary's cross. It was here that He terminated the old creation which breeds divisions, and strife, and rivalry, and jealousy, and sectarianism, and pride (the pride that prides itself on its imagined humility). In the power of the Resurrection "the new man" (new creation) was brought into being. "If any man be in Christ, he is a new creature [creation]: old things are passed away; behold, all things are become new" (II Corinthians 5:17). And, of course, here the constraining, dominating force of one's life is love. "The love of Christ," says Paul in the same breath, "constraineth us . . ." (II Corinthians 5:14).

37

THE CROSS —
THE POWER OF GOD

ONE WOULD NOT naturally associate power with the cross. God's power surely is to be found in the creation and direction and maintenance of the three hundred million universes of which astronomers speak today. Indeed, but that higher power released in the moral order for the redemption of man at enmity with God because of sin, springs from Calvary's cross. For the weakness of God, Paul says, is stronger than men, and the foolishness of God is wiser than men. "For my thoughts are not your thoughts, neither are your ways my ways, saith the Lord. For as the heavens are higher than the earth, so are my ways higher than your ways, and my thoughts than your thoughts" (Isaiah 55:8, 9).

There is a variety of translations in the many versions of the New Testament of I Corinthians 1:18. I have chosen the one in the *American Standard Version.* "For the word of the cross is to them that perish foolishness; but unto us who are saved it is the power of God." Never was there such a display of the power, and wisdom, and love, and righteousness of God as in that hour. The Lord God Most High threw in all that He had. Nothing was withheld. Wisdom spent itself; love exhausted all her treasures; power gave all; righteousness could do no more.

Look not at sunset's splendor with skies bathed in golden hues; look not at the beauties of gardens aglow with lilies, daffodils, roses, and hyacinths; look not at the awful majesty of trees, and mountains, and mighty streams; look not at some

stern moral code, whether Biblical or otherwise. Would you
see the glory of God in its most complete, its most exalted, its
maximum effulgence? You need not wait until heaven be your
home and the throne of God before you. Look now, look with
the sinner's grateful gaze. Look at the cross and see the eternal
Christ who by the word of His power upholds all things; see
Him made your sin and your curse there on the tree that you
might be free from sin's awful guilt and condemnation. Should
you be so blessed as to see by the illumination of the Holy Spirit
what the wisdom and love of God have placed there for you,
nothing will ever again enthrall your enraptured soul. With
Paul you will cry, "God forbid that I should glory save in the
cross of our Lord Jesus Christ."

The word "power" in the Greek is *dunamis,* from which we
derive our word "dynamite." Truly the word of the cross is the
dynamite of God. No such power to break men's hearts, hard
as flint because of pride, will ever be known whether on earth
or in Heaven. When the Holy Spirit, whose function it is to glorify
Christ and to take the things that are His (and nothing is so
truly His as the cross) to reveal them to men, when, I repeat,
the Holy Spirit opens this word — the word of the cross which
is the dynamite of God — to some needy soul, something takes
place akin to what happened when on the cross our Lord cried,
"It is finished." There was an earthquake, the rocks were rent,
and graves were opened. The rocks of human pride are rent;
self-satisfaction and bigotry quake; and the grave dug deep by
lust, and greed, and self-love, is opened.

Dynamite removes great barriers, mighty granite block-
ades, where a highway for progress is being opened up. Never
was there such an insurmountable mountain as that which man's
sin had raised. There was no hope of ever being able to drill
through, or surmount such a barrier to God's holy presence.
No one dared touch Sinai's flaming Mount with its revelation
of God's holiness and its law for man, lest he die. Indeed, the
wages of sin is death whether written in the Bible or not. How
surmount this terrible barrier more impregnable than a thousand
Gibraltars? Behold, the dynamite of the cross! Love found a
way, which righteousness, even God's, could not (because it

would not) countermand. "Look and live" still holds good. The door is open which all the demons of hell, nor their prince, the "roaring lion" of Peter's epistle, can ever close. It is the door of mercy opened at Calvary to all believing, repentant sinners.

Then, too dynamite destroys; it blasts to pieces mighty fortresses. There is a citadel of pride in man's heart that is strong, that though hell be its lot, will never surrender. Law cannot move it. The mightiest angel is impotent before its strength. Prisons and torture and death have been defied over and over by the children of men, rather than to fail to fulfill its demands. It is the very strength and glory of man, *that is to say, man the sinner in revolt against God.* But there is power that dissolves this mountain of pride. The citadel (so as not to change our figure) cannot withstand it. We see it in Paul, erstwhile Saul of Tarsus. A prouder Pharisee could not have been found. He was a tiger "breathing out threatenings and slaughter." But the blinding vision on the road to Damascus did the work. Hear him (pride gone) saying: "I am crucified together with Christ." Now Christ is on the throne. Paul is willing to be nothing, just so Christ be glorified. The dynamite of the cross did it.

The very first promise in all the Scripture gave it out (Genesis 3:15). The Seed of the woman (Christ the Lord) would bruise the head of that old serpent, the devil. The blow was struck at Calvary. The dynamite was released through the cross. Oh, how the prince of this world and his hosts must have shuddered and cried out in immeasurable dismay as they realized that that which they thought was the end of the claims of this pretender Prince (for them pretender) was really the end of theirs. Their authority, based as it was on man's sin (removed, praise God, at Calvary), had been shattered. Shattered in a way so wonderful, inasmuch as the broken law to which they pointed and which gave them authority had been fulfilled in the death of the representative Man, so wonderful, I repeat, as shall forever stand the scrutiny of all created beings either good or bad without the possibility of a flaw or a stain ever being found.

The word of the cross is the power of God. The preaching of the cross is the wisdom of God (I Corinthians 1:24). For lo, John the apostle hears a loud voice in heaven saying: "Now is come salvation, and strength, and the kingdom of our God, and the power of his Christ: for the accuser of our brethren is cast down, which accused them before our God day and night. And they overcame him by the blood of the Lamb" (Revelation 12:10, 11).

38

BEARING ABOUT THE DYING OF JESUS

THERE IS A WORD of deepest significance, as we continue to go through the Scriptures in an ever fuller unveiling of the cross of Christ, which we must not pass over. It is found in the second epistle to the Corinthians where the apostle makes the amazing statement that as Christians we always bear about in our bodies the dying of the Lord Jesus, this, in order that the life also of Jesus might be made manifest in our bodies. Whereupon Paul goes on to say: "For we which live are alway delivered unto death for Jesus' sake, that the life also of Jesus might be made manifest in our mortal flesh" (II Corinthians 4: 10, 11). So not only is the cross paramount in the Scriptures. It runs straight through the Christian life, from first to last "the dying of Jesus" is to be borne, for thus also is the life of Jesus made manifest.

As I have found through commentaries and different versions of the Scriptures there seems to be a tendency to tone down this word of the apostle's, as if it could not possibly mean what it says. The perils of the Christian life in that age of persecution, the constant threat of death, the losses coupled with the testimony of Jesus, the privations and sicknesses especially in the case of the one who writes, are what the apostle has in mind, so we are told, as he writes these astounding words.

The immediate context ("we are troubled on every side, yet not distressed, we are perplexed, but not in despair, persecuted, but not forsaken, cast down, but not destroyed, always bearing about . . .") seems to indicate that such indeed is the apostle's thought. But to get at his deepest meaning, this which

140

is so repugnant to the "flesh" (who wants to bear about in his body the dying of Jesus?) must be taken in the light of a more complete context. We must view it as related to Paul's basic concept regarding the Christian life, the warp and woof of his theology as regards the believer's position. He is identified with his Lord. What happened to Christ as representative Man, the Federal Head of the new creation, happened to him. Christ was crucified; then he, too. Christ died; he shares his Redeemer's tomb. Christ was quickened; so was he. Christ arose from the dead; he arose (in spirit) with Him. Christ ascended; nothing less can be said of the Christian. Christ sits at the right hand of God: the believer has been made to sit together with Him in heavenly places (see Romans 6; Ephesians 2:4-6; Colossians 3:1-4).

The Christian, in a word, is utterly, absolutely, and forever identified with his Lord and Saviour Jesus Christ. It could not be otherwise; for if Jesus bore my sins in His body on the tree, then that is where I am. What you see there, in a sense, is not Jesus at all. You see me; for that is my sin. If Jesus stood in my shoes (a more perfect identification could not be conceived) then I am identified with Him; I stand in His shoes. His exaltation is mine — enthroned together with Him, as in the Weymouth translation (Ephesians 2:4-6).

What we have in II Corinthians 4:10, 11 comes as a logical sequence. Would you have the life of Jesus manifest in your body? Then you must share with Him His dying. We have said in a former chapter that the union of the Christian with his Saviour was not really effected save in Christ's death and Resurrection. But this inevitably brings him to a vital sharing of his Lord's dying. For could he be one with Christ, in such a world as this, and not share with Him His dying, or if you prefer, His sufferings?

Ah, yes, we find ourselves in deep water. But who would wish to be elsewhere with such a Saviour, truly infinitely adorable? This awful fact shows up repeatedly in Paul's epistles in its bearing on his own experience. (See Paul, the pattern for all Christians, I Timothy 1:16.) "Who now rejoice in my sufferings for you, and fill up that which is behind of the afflictions of Christ in my flesh for his body's sake, which is the church"

(Colossians 1:24). Or as it is in Philippians where Paul speaks of his great love for Christ, willing to lose all things and count them but dung that he might win Christ, though being found in Him meant sharing in the fellowship of His sufferings, being made in the power of His Resurrection, conformable unto His death (Philippians 3:8-10). Lest this be looked upon as a personal peculiarity of Paul, let us look to Romans 8:17, where our being joint-heirs of God with Christ is conditioned upon our suffering with Him.

Indeed it is strong language, this which we find in II Corinthians 4:10, 11. But "bearing about in the body the dying of the Lord Jesus," and always being delivered unto death for His sake, exactly states the case for those who are willing to go all the way with Jesus, renouncing their own life to have only His. They enter into the fellowship of His sufferings. Some, like "Praying Hyde of India," whose ceaseless groanings in the Spirit brought revival to the church of India, have literally died of a broken heart. Space forbids an enumeration of the Church's martyrs ("Ye shall be my witnesses" of Acts 1:8 — our English word martyr is taken from the Greek word for witness). To be identified, I repeat, with Christ in such a world as this, means the cross.

But this is not all. It is thus that "the rivers of living water" begin to flow. The cross is the way to the fullness of the Spirit (unless we want a counterfeit — "try the spirits"). It is that the life of Jesus might also be made manifest in our mortal flesh. Jesus Himself went this way. He is indeed "the way." The cross, death, Resurrection, Ascension, Pentecost. A "Pentecost" coming any other way is a counterfeit.

"Always bearing about in the body the dying of the Lord Jesus."

39

THE CROSS
AND THE HOLY SPIRIT

THE EPISTLE TO THE GALATIANS is the most intensely Pauline of the apostle's writings. There is nothing in the New Testament that so reveals Paul as this. The epistle is autobiographical. Paul tells of his conversion and of how, as a Jew, he came to such devotion to his Lord, breaking utterly with Judaism and considering himself crucified together with Christ to have no life of his own — no life save that of the Christ within. It is no longer I, says Paul, but ever and only Christ.

There is terrific conflict. Paul is beside himself. He cannot brook this thing. He pronounces a curse upon those who would pervert the Gospel. Even though it be an angel from heaven preaching a gospel other than the one Paul and his companions have preached, "let him be anathema" (Galatians 1:6-8).

Paul does not know what to think. He cannot conceive how these Galatians could have gone aside, turning their backs on Christ in favor of Jewish legalism (circumcision). Someone has bewitched the Galatian Christians. "O foolish Galatians, who hath bewitched you?" exclaims the apostle. He feels obligated to use the severest language at his command, to reprove these converts of his. He goes so far as to say he stands in doubt of them, not knowing whether he can still address them as brethren. He gives them to understand that if they go through with this which the Judaizers from Jerusalem are seeking by all means to foist upon them, they have fallen from grace.

It is not for me, fortunately, to discuss whether a Christian can fall from grace. What I am getting at is the clue to Paul's wrath. Is it justifiable? Is his indignation really holy?

We find upon analysis that it is more than justifiable, inasmuch as the Galatians under the spell of the Judaizers' clever talk were belittling the cross of Christ. They were saying, in effect, that what the Saviour had wrought on Calvary's cross was not sufficient as the grounds of their salvation; they must add Judaistic practices (Moses added to Christ). Paul is highly sensitive as regards the glory of the cross. Any personal offense he would be glad to pardon; but to infer that the Redeemer's awful consummation of the work of redemption wrought at so great a cost on the accursed tree where He shed his most precious blood for the remission of sins and the justification of the sinner, was something which needed to be improved upon, or added to, was too much for Paul. "God forbid," he stoutly declares to these foolish Galatians, "that I should glory, save in the cross of our Lord Jesus Christ" (Galatians 6:14). "If you must," seems to be the implication, "you Gentiles may glory in the Mosaic system, circumcision and all the rest; as for me, Jew that I am, I shall glory in nothing save my Redeemer's cross."

As Paul draws his epistle to a close, he confronts the problem of the Christian's walk in the Spirit. "Received ye the Spirit," he asks, "by the works of the law, or by the hearing of faith?" The apostle's answer is clear: "Christ hath redeemed us from the curse of the law, being made a curse for us: for it is written, Cursed is every one that hangeth on a tree: that the blessing of Abraham might come on the Gentiles through Jesus Christ, that we might receive the promise of the Spirit through faith" (Galatians 3:13, 14).

Indeed it is by faith, but it is most emphatically stated, the ground of our faith being the cross and not the law. It is because the Lord Jesus Christ has removed the curse that rested upon us due to our sin, that through His passion and death it might all be taken away, that we might receive the blessing promised to Abraham: "In thee shall all the families of the earth be blessed" (Genesis 12:3). That is to say, that we might receive the promise of the Spirit through faith.

The indwelling of the Holy Spirit, the Christian being a temple of God, is so vitally associated with the cross, that for Paul, the Holy Spirit leads to the cross, as the cross leads to the Holy Spirit. The apostle would laugh at the idea of having the fullness of the Spirit apart from the cross. He would take us to Romans 6 and affirm that identification with Christ in death and in resurrection is the condition, *sine qua non*. Why, were the Holy Spirit to give power apart from the cross, He would betray Christ to glorify whom He came! For Christ the Lord took the old creation with Him to the cross. How can the Spirit energize what Christ terminated at Calvary? He can only fill on the ground of a participation of the cross where the Lord put to an end the dominion of the old life of pride which is man's by nature (Adamic).

In the closing chapter of the Galatian epistle, Paul goes into this matter with such force as to settle it for all time. He tells us that the flesh lusteth against the Spirit, and the Spirit against the flesh. He makes it very clear what the works of the flesh are: "Adultery, fornication, uncleanness, lasciviousness, idolatry, witchcraft, hatred, variance, emulations, wrath, strife, seditions, heresies, envyings, murders, drunkenness, revellings, and such like" (Galatians 5:19-21). He is no less clear as to what the fruit of the Spirit is: "Love, joy, peace, longsuffering, gentleness, goodness, faith, meekness, temperance," against which, Paul says, there is no law (Galatians 5:22, 23).

Now the crowning word of the passage (Galatians 5) is verse 24 where we are told that they that are Christ's have crucified the flesh with the affections and lusts. Thus the great apostle to the Gentiles categorically affirms, if I may so put it, that the Christian is in a position to live in the Spirit and to walk in the Spirit only as "the flesh" is crucified. Indeed the Spirit works through the cross, and the cross issues in the Spirit. The Holy Spirit and the cross are really one. The Spirit can work in no other way.

40

FROM THE THRONE TO THE CROSS

THE APOSTLE IN Philippians 2 follows the Lord Jesus our Saviour from the throne straight to the cross. It reads as if for this very purpose He had come. And, indeed, it was even so.

I shall take the passage as it is found in the American Standard Version. "Have this mind in you, which was also in Christ Jesus: who, existing in the form of God, counted not the being on an equality with God a thing to be grasped, but emptied himself, taking the form of a servant, being made in the likeness of men; and being found in fashion as a man, he humbled himself, becoming obedient even unto death, yea, the death of the cross" (Philippians 2:5-8).

It will be well for us to pause and take our breath, before quoting further from Paul. For this has, indeed, left us breathless. There is nothing more overwhelming in all nature, in all the universe, in all the moral history of God. Here we have Him surpassing Himself, so to speak, and coming to His highest stature.

Of course, it is, as Paul writes to the Corinthians, foolishness. Tell this to some man wise in worldly lore, but deprived of the grace of God, and he will laugh at you. The Saviour said what would happen if we were to cast our pearls before swine. I am only quoting Jesus our Lord; so do not say I am harsh. It is He who could be very severe, in the midst of His incomparable loveliness.

Indeed, it is foolishness, until the Spirit of God may have opened your eyes to see. And then you behold the wonder of all the ages. You could not before conceive of one being so good. That the One by whom all things were made in Heaven and upon earth should leave His throne and stoop so low (from the throne to a criminal's cross of ignominy and shame) out of love for a sinful race — well, you could give the philosopher a million years to think, and the moralist no less time to surmise about right and wrong, and the statesman even more days to ponder over law and order, and crime and its punishment, and yet, in the most amazing flight of the imagination possible for man, nothing of this nature could be remotely conceived. This is of God. Take it as such, else it will ever be foolishness.

And yet love has been known to do unheard-of things. It is capable of a nobility such as has stirred the breast of poets and bards. A mother's love, a patriot's love, a lover's love, a reformer's love: men have died for country, yea, for every noble cause of earth.

But this is as different withal as midday from midnight. You cannot find ground for comparisons. You never would be able to establish any real likeness worthy of the name. This, for the reason that not the need of a soul or a nation are involved. You may, perhaps, have suffered for the sins of another. However, none but the God-Man, Jesus Christ our Lord, could bear the burden of the sin of the world and make atonement.

How strange, however, for Paul says it in one word, and makes no effort to go beyond. He simply states the fact which only faith (the fruit of immeasurable gratitude) can grasp. "Him who knew no sin he [the Father] made to be sin on our behalf that we might become the righteousness of God in him" (II Corinthians 5:21). There you have it. Nothing else tells the story. This is why He left His throne and went all the way to Calvary. Your sin, my sin, the sins of the world could not lightly be forgiven. A cheap forgiveness would shame the government of God, and what's more, would corrupt man even more. Sin must be dealt with as God's law declares, let theologians say what they will. Hence the cross, not to appease God's wrath, but to give free rein to His love while at the same time all the requirements of Heaven's righteous government (righteous as only God can be) might be duly executed.

But we must return to Philippians 2 if we would come to a full appraisal of all this. We read: "Wherefore also God hath highly exalted him, and gave him a name which is above every name; that in the name of Jesus every knee should bow, of things in heaven, and things on earth, and things under the earth, and that every tongue should confess that Jesus Christ is Lord, to the glory of God the Father" (Philippians 2:9-11).

Again we are breathless. He who stooped so low (never were such depths of ignominy and shame sounded) was raised to heights of glory and majesty and power which would beggar the imagination of seraphims, and cherubims, and all the hosts of Heaven.

Nothing but the empty tomb, Resurrection, Ascension, and Pentecost, could ever have offset Calvary's shame and seeming defeat. Nothing but the glory of the Resurrection, and the victory of the Ascension, and the blessed outpouring of the Holy Spirit, could ever have wiped out the ignominy. These are but the stepping-stones, of which "Wherefore also God hath highly exalted him, and gave him a name which is above every name; that in the name of Jesus every knee should bow, of things in heaven, and things on earth, and things under the earth, and that every tongue should confess that Jesus Christ is Lord, to the glory of God the Father" is the only logical sequence. The one has no meaning without the other.

Oh, what glory would be the Christian's and what power would be seen in the Church if this mind which was in Christ were to truly characterize both. The greed for ecclesiastical power would be gone, and the humility of Jesus would be paramount. The Church would overcome the world, and not the world the Church. There would be no need for showy, superficial architecture in a vying for first place. He who raised up Jesus and set Him at His own right hand would also raise up the Christian and give him the place which judicially he already possesses. But his judicial standing according to Ephesians 2:4-6 can only become actual in experience as the cross is applied. The verdict of Calvary, which is God's, must be ratified in the manner of Galatians 5 where we read that they that are Christ's have crucified the flesh with its affections and lusts.

41

THE CROSS —
THE CHURCH'S ALTAR

"WE HAVE AN ALTAR," wrote the sacred writer in the epistle to the Hebrews (Hebrews 13:10). In verse 8 of the same chapter we read: "Jesus Christ the same yesterday, and to day, and for ever."

Here we have the theme of this wonderful epistle: Jesus Christ, the Church's High Priest — and the altar. Now the altar is the cross, to whose glory the epistle is dedicated. There were Hebrew Christians turning back to Jewish practices, the altar, the tabernacle, the priests, the sacrifices, in a search for peace. The Hebrew epistle rings the changes, and with what zeal and authority, and wisdom. No, says the writer, a thousand times no. "We have an altar." We have an high priest. We have a sure means of approach to God. Our High Priest has removed every barrier. When Christ died on the cross the veil of the temple was rent. We enter into the holiest by this new and living way. We may enter boldly by the blood of Jesus (Hebrews 10:19).

Let us briefly scan these salient points, as presented in the epistle to the Hebrews. First of all, we have an high priest. "Seeing then that we have a great high priest, that is passed into the heavens, Jesus the Son of God, let us hold fast our profession. For we have not an high priest which cannot be touched with the feeling of our infirmities; but was in all points tempted like as we are, yet without sin" (Hebrews 4:14, 15).

Let us now ask, who then is this great high priest? Is he capable of dealing with sin and making things right before the Most High God? Hebrews tells us that He is both God and Man.

No one of less stature could deal with so vast a problem. So truly God is He that the Father addresses Him saying: "Thy throne, O God, is for ever and ever: a sceptre of righteousness is the sceptre of thy kingdom" (Hebrews 1:8). And so very man is He that it is written: "Forasmuch then as the children are partakers of flesh and blood, he also himself likewise took part of the same" (behold Bethlehem's manger) (Hebrews 2:14). So truly man that He was tempted in all points like as we yet without sin (Hebrews 2:14-18, 4:15). Verily this One was fitted, fully equipped for so great a task.

But what was the task our faithful High Priest undertook in our behalf? It takes one's breath and leaves one overwhelmed with awe. "Who [Christ] being the brightness of his glory, and the express image of his person, and upholding all things by the word of his power, when he had by himself purged our sins [behold the glory of the cross], sat down on the right hand of the Majesty on high" (Hebrews 1:3). Or if one would wish a more explicit word: "Now once in the end of the world hath he appeared to put away sin by the sacrifice of himself" (Hebrews 9:26). Our blessed High Priest is both Priest and altar; He is the Lamb sacrificed and the Priest sacrificing. Little wonder that He should say that He would remember our sins no more (Hebrews 10:17). Having taken them away so effectively, they shall be remembered no more forever.

But this is not all. Priests must intercede for needy souls. Wonder of wonders, blessed truth of all truths of Holy Writ: "This man [Jesus Christ], because he continueth ever, hath an unchangeable priesthood. Wherefore he is able also to save them to the uttermost that come unto God by him, seeing he ever liveth to make intercession for them" (Hebrews 7:24, 25). Think of having such a one as Christ Jesus the Lord (high priest over the house of God, Hebrews 10:21) praying for you, ever interceding! Is there anything in heaven or on earth that could more truly establish a believer in the faith and make perfect his assurance?

There is more; the enemy of souls, the devil, is no match for our adorable High Priest. Why, through death (again it is the cross) He destroyed him who had the power of death, that is to say, the devil (Hebrews 2:14). But is not the devil as active as ever if not more so? Yes, but for the one who is in Christ he has been brought to nought and rendered ineffective (*The Amplified Bible*). The Christian can trample the dragon underfoot and declare him a defeated foe, such was the achievement of his Great High Priest who through His wondrous death and His glorious Resurrection stripped the devil of his authority and cancelled his rights.

Could more be wished? Is there still some great need? Be it what it may, our Great High Priest has the answer. Why, we are told in chapter 12 that as Aaron, Israel's high priest, carried the twelve tribes upon his heart, their names inscribed upon the breastplate he bore as he appeared before God in their behalf, so our High Priest, no mere type but the fulfillment of all Old Testament types and prophecies, bears with Himself to the very throne of God all true believers. For we are assured in the epistle to the Hebrews that we have already arrived. Where Jesus the Lord is, there are His own. "Ye are come unto mount Sion, and unto the city of the living God, the heavenly Jerusalem, and to an innumerable company of angels, to the general assembly and church of the firstborn, which are written in heaven, and to God the Judge of all, and to the spirits of just men made perfect, and to Jesus the mediator of the new covenant" (Hebrews 12:22-24). It does not say we shall come, but we are come. So effective is our High Priest.

Our part, what is it? "Let us go forth therefore unto him without the camp, bearing his reproach" (Hebrews 13:13).

"Wherefore Jesus also, that he might sanctify the people with his own blood, suffered without the gate" (Hebrews 13:12).

Who could resist such a Saviour and not follow Him without the camp, bearing His reproach?

42

THE BLOOD – FOREVER CLEANSING

IT IS NOT POSSIBLE to close this section of our theme without pausing over a word which John, the beloved disciple, gives us in his first epistle. There is perfect harmony throughout the Scriptures regarding the immeasurable significance of the cross of Christ—a glory that can never be fathomed. Let us just set the word off, as it were, in a frame all its own. It is so exceedingly precious.

"But if we walk in the light, as he is in the light, we have fellowship one with another, and the blood of Jesus Christ his Son cleanseth us from all sin" (I John 1:7).

Now the amazing fact regarding the efficacy of our Lord's sacrifice effected on Calvary's cross, as here set forth by John the apostle, is that it is forever operative. The verb "cleanse" in the Greek is in the present active tense. The blood never ceases to cleanse the Christian who is walking in the light. Could anything be found more perfectly designed to keep him walking in victory?

Now as for the common Biblical expression, which John also employs, many moderns have felt that it is out of date. There must be some better way of stating the facts in relation to the cross of Christ. This that the blood of Christ cleanseth, surely there must be a way less offensive of expressing this matter. Not a few feel this way. My answer is that "the offense of the cross," to use Paul's expression, remains. There will never be found a way of getting around that. It *is* terribly offensive to the sinner, this fact, forever reiterated in Holy Writ, that Christ died for his sins: for the cross is the measure of sin's heinousness.

Here his sin is photographed, and what it cost to remove it. Offensive? To be sure. But oh, the glory and blessedness once the fact is accepted and Christ is received as Saviour.

What I am getting at is the fact that the offense is, after all, not in the cross but in man — the sinner. Once there is a willingness to face up to the cross for the exposing of the infinite shame of one's sin, there really is no problem. There comes not only a willingness, but immeasurable joy and satisfaction in the use of this Biblical term so repellent to many. Needless to say, it is not an actual material application of the precious blood of Christ so copiously shed on the cross. It is the appropriation in simple faith of that which no other word so effectively, may I say so eloquently, expresses as "the blood of Christ," namely, the sacrifice effected on Calvary's cross for the putting away of the sins of the world.

So let us be willing to use the language (no other so expressive will ever be found) which God has seen fit to give us in His Holy Word. I happen to be reading the life of the great Quaker philosopher and Christian, Thomas R. Kelly. Trained at Harvard, having taught philosophy in the Far East in Hawaii, serving in Germany where he also studied, and directed Quaker relief activities, he at last returned to Haverford for his closing professorship. I have been moved to the deepest depths of my soul by his *Testament of Devotion*. Here now is the fact which falls in so beautifully with my argument, if I may call it that. Thomas R. Kelly shocked his high-brow students (it was in the closing days of his ministry, for his professorship was truly a ministry) by his constant use of the words, "the blood of Christ." The great philosopher, a most devoted Christian, could find no better way of expressing the efficacy of the Redeemer's sacrifice. Truly the precious blood of Christ not only cleanseth, but is forever cleansing the Christian from all sin.

Of course, there is a condition. John says, "if we walk in the light." Willful sins, as the apostle indicates in the verses that follow, should be confessed, and then comes forgiveness and cleansing.

Now I John 1:7 with its promise of an ever-present and ever-active cleansing by virtue of the blood of Christ, strikes at the heart of the Christian's ever present need. How live in unbroken communion with the Father of Lights ("Holy, Holy, Holy, Lord God Almighty") when in a world such as this, his garments are forever being besmirched? Not only from without come the stains, but from within, for as John goes on to say, "If we say that we have no sin, we deceive ourselves, and the truth is not in us" (I John 1:8).

The answer is: the blood of Christ is forever cleansing us. You say, but how can that be? May I be permitted to draw from nature a simple analogy, also a work of God — one from grace, the other from nature. The eye is forever washing its face; we are not aware of the fact. Secretions that flow over this delicate organ keep it clean. The fluid with its microscopic trash runs out of a duct, draining through a delicate channel at the eye's base. So the eye, which cannot put up with any dirt, as it were, is being cleansed, moment by moment.

But the soul is even more delicate. It was made for purity, and only in the realm of purity can it truly live. The slightest blemish, how it irritates. Sin is as foreign to the Christian, born again with Christ enthroned, as the filth of some cesspool to a lamb freshly washed.

How wonderful: the blood of Christ is forever cleansing. The virtue of the cross is forever being applied. The Holy Spirit sees to that — "if we walk in the light."

This was the word which enabled Frances Havergal, one of the church's sweetest hymn writers, to march into the promised land of a life of perennial victory in Christ. She had long been a burdened Christian bowed down with shame because of her many faults. But one day she read in her Greek New Testament I John 1:7, and discovered that the blood of Christ was forever cleansing. It was one of the greatest discoveries of her life. It was the end of sorrow. It was the dawn of a new day. Her communion with God became uninterrupted. Her joy was unspeakable and full of glory. When she was called home, her Bible lay open on the casket at I John 1:7.

Part Four

THE CROSS
IN THE
APOCALYPSE

43

'UNTO HIM THAT WASHED US'

THERE IS A GREAT HARMONY in the Scriptures, a sublime oneness of purpose. No sooner do we step over into the realm of the Apocalypse than Calvary looms up before us. We are taken at once to the cross.

One would think that now this glorying in the cross of Christ would give way to beauties, and excellencies, and glories of another order. In the Apocalypse we are caught up with the Seer of Patmos into the heavenlies. It is no longer the kingdom of earth with its sorry need of redemption. It is now the Kingdom of our God and of His Christ. It is the City whose streets are of gold, and whose very foundations are garnished with all manner of precious stones, nor can these fitly symbolize such glory. Can we not now leave the cross and gaze upon something yet more wonderful?

The answer of the Apocalypse is most emphatically, No! On the contrary, there is a turning back to Calvary for a yet more complete unveiling of the cross. The sea-divers who in the Scriptures have combed the deeps of the ocean of God's love for the pearl of great price now are outwitted by the Seer of Patmos who plunges into depths never before known only to come forth with glories of the Redeemer's cross which can be fully appreciated only in Heaven.

"Unto him that loved us, and washed us from our sins [the *American Standard Version* gives it "loosed"] in his own blood, and hath made us kings and priests unto God and his Father; to him be glory and dominion for ever and ever. Amen" (Revelation 1:6). So the dominant note of the heavenly symphony is

159

struck at once. And to this glorious note all is attuned throughout the entire book.

But surely there is no need of the cross in Heaven. The cross of Christ is for sinners, earth dwellers hoping, as the pilgrim in Bunyan's fair vision who leaves his burden at the foot of the cross, to arrive at the Celestial City. The Apocalypse most categorically declares that the cross is even more for Heaven, declaring that millions of redeemed souls find nothing so worthy of their praises nor anything they more rapturously explore.

We shall discover as we move across the pages of this amazing book whose mysteries so baffle Christian scholars, that the central Mystery is no mystery at all, for the secret is out. It is Christ in His ascended, glorified, enthroned Person. It is the same Jesus of Nazareth; it is the rejected, crucified Messiah, the Christ of God come at last, via Calvary, the empty tomb, and ascension to the throne of God, to reign forever with all authority given to Him both in Heaven and upon earth. John falls at His feet as one dead, for His countenance is as the sun that shineth in his strength. Who can gaze upon the noonday sun when in its meridian glory?

The Apocalypse may have much we can never fully fathom, so prolific is its symbolism, so lofty its themes, and so great its grandeur. However, its message eclipsing all else is Christ Himself in His ascended glory. He is the Alpha and Omega of the Scriptures, as well as of all creation, and for that matter of history itself. "And every creature," says John, "which is in heaven, and on earth, and under the earth, and such as are in the sea, and all that are in them, heard I saying, Blessing, and honour, and glory, and power, be unto him that sitteth upon the throne, and unto the Lamb for ever and ever" (Revelation 5:13).

Now this brings us to our theme, *The Cross Through the Scriptures*. What baffles us and leaves us breathless with wonder and awe is the fact that as Christ our Lord is revealed to us in the Apocalypse He is clothed in the garments of His sacrificial glory. It is as the Lamb slain. It is in terms of His cross. It is as the One who was dead, and lo, is alive forevermore. It is with the marks of the awful tree boldly displayed. It is thus that He is identified. (There are false Christs, do not forget. See Matthew 24:23, 24.)

Now just what does this mean? The following chapters are the answer. But we may say in this preview that it means over and above all else that the moral verities engendered through the cross are eternal and are to be forever conserved in the throne. This will be expounded more fully later. Suffice it to say for the present that the cross is eternally associated with the throne.

It is as if a king should say to some poor wretch condemned to die on the gallows who had appealed for mercy: "I am sorry, I cannot pardon you. As king of the realm I must be the first in establishing and honoring her just laws. But there is one thing I can do. I can die for you, and so the law will be fulfilled." Let us presume that so it comes to pass. And now the analogy breaks down. However, we will presume nevertheless that the good king, having died for said evildoer now arises from his grave and returns again to occupy the throne he had left. Ah, but it is a different throne now. Its glory has been enhanced a million times. Such a throne was never conceived. The king, before good and just, is seen in a light and a glory so great as to ravish the hearts of a hundred million subjects. The king seen in the light of the gallows he bore for another, and clothed in resurrection splendor, is now not only obeyed but receives adoration never to be measured. His kingdom has been purified, for the very worst are humbled and transformed before such justice.

The illustration may be crude as all such are when aimed to throw light on God's supreme glory, the cross. Yet we shall see as we enter the sacred realm of the Apocalypse, where we have our adorable King and Redeemer, the Lord Jesus Christ, manifested in His Resurrection-Ascension Majesty, that this is exactly what happened when the King of glory died on the cross and rose again. Of course it is the same throne, and yet not the same. The enthroned King bears the marks of His cross and Heaven looks deep into their meaning and will do so forever. The glory of the throne has been enhanced a million times!

44

A LAMB SLAIN IN THE THRONE

THERE IS NOTHING more wonderful, more significant for the children of men than what is found in chapter 5 of the closing book of the Bible. Little wonder that this book should be called "Revelation." How tremendous this that John beheld on the Isle of Patmos when for him a door was opened in Heaven and a voice was heard saying, "Come up hither."

He tells us that he wept much as no one was found worthy to open the mysterious book with its seven seals, the symbolic book in which were found the judgments of God; neither in heaven nor on earth was anyone found who could open the seven seals. He is told not to weep but to look upon the Lion of the tribe of Judah. John lifts his eyes to the throne, and what does he see? A Lamb "in the midst of the throne," standing as though it had been slain" (Revelation 5:6).

Now the song which the apostle hears (John calls it a new song) is this: "Worthy art thou to take the book and to open the seals thereof; for thou wast slain, and hast redeemed us to God by thy blood out of every kindred, and tongue, and people, and nation" (Revelation 5:9).

The language of the apostle is most majestic. He goes on saying: "I beheld, and heard the voice of many angels round about the throne . . . and the number of them was ten thousand times ten thousand, and thousands of thousands, saying with a loud voice, Worthy is the Lamb that was slain to receive power, and riches, and wisdom, and strength, and honour, and glory, and blessing." It is before the Lamb that the four and twenty elders (no doubt a symbolic number representing the redeemed of both the Old and the New Testament dispensations) fall down to worship, as it is written, every one of them with harps, and golden vials, which are the prayers of the saints.

And so we are face to face with the astounding fact that the hosts of Heaven which cannot be numbered, with joyful song forever commemorate the blessed Saviour's achievement effected on the cruel tree of Calvary. They find nothing so worthy of their praise, nothing so commending of their worship, nothing so fitting an object of their adoration as the Lamb that was slain. All the splendors of Heaven are eclipsed by the matchless splendor of the cross. Ah, it is the wounds of the Crucified-Risen Lord. Where else would the blessed redeemed, gathered about the throne of God, look for the fulfillment of their ecstasy and their rapture?

It falls to us now to draw the conclusions which logically follow all this.

First, the redeemed of Heaven, bathed in the very light of God, are in a position to look, as we in our mortal frame cannot, deep into the Saviour's awful sacrifice consummated on Calvary's cross. They can appreciate more fully its immeasurable glory and blessedness in relation to the needs of sinful mankind under the curse of a broken law which can do no more than pronounce for man an unspeakable doom. They need no one to tell them why Paul should have said, "God forbid that I should glory, save in the cross of our Lord Jesus Christ" (Galatians 6:14). They know as even he could not have known.

In the second place, the song of the redeemed, glorying as they do in the Lamb that was slain, throws a flood of light on the economy, or should I say, the manner of the workings of the government of God. Thrones are for government. Whatever the government of God may have been, it is now mediated by the Lamb of God, slain for sinners. His blood, precious beyond words, cleanseth from all sin. In a word, what constitutes the right, the legal right, if I may so put it, to be in the presence of God, in the midst of a glory earth-dwellers can never fathom? The redeemed in Heaven say that it is the cross of Christ. "Worthy art thou, O Lamb of God, for thou wast slain and hast redeemed us to God by thy blood."

They do not say, "Our tears, and struggles, and labors, and righteousness brought us here." They glory in Him who for them wrought righteousness, yea, fulfilling the claims of God's holy law on the cross. They find in His blood the ground of their redemption. If these chapters have failed to make manifest the fact that this is the testimony of the Scriptures from first to last, they have been written in vain.

There is a third deduction. Where are we to look for the supreme manifestation of the glory of God? Theologians talk about the natural attributes of God, they say, such as His omnipotence, His omniscience, His omnipresence; and the moral attributes, such as His justice, His mercy, His faithfulness, His truth, and His never changing love. As it is with man, whose greatness, if such be his, is not found in his power, but in his goodness, so it is with God. His true greatness does not lie in the fact that He could speak and three hundred million universes with worlds as numerous as the grains of sand on the shores of the seas should be born.

His supreme glory is found in the fact that His goodness is so great that the Son of God by whom all things were made would leave His throne and glory and take upon Himself the form of a man that He might die on an accursed tree, where He was made sin, all in order to free man from guilt and condemnation and so fit him for Heaven, the Heaven he had lost because of sin. Now this need not be told to the redeemed of Heaven. They see it as we can never see it here on earth. For them, no occupation so in keeping with their deepest passion as to sing the praises of the Lamb that was slain that they might be redeemed unto God by His blood.

And finally, we conclude that the very life of Heaven is now based on the cross. There will be more of this later. But we close even now pointing to the fact that though sin first broke out in *Heaven* before ever it appeared on *earth*, it will never again break out in mansions of light where the great theme of all, whether of angels or saints, is the glory of the Lamb that was slain. Not only has earth been redeemed (it breaks your heart, for there are many who do not believe and so do not receive) by the infinite virtue of the cross of Christ; but Heaven as well has been secured for ever and ever from any further outbreak of evil. (See Hebrews 9:18-23.)

It was the pride of that great angel, Lucifer, the son of the morning, which brought sin into God's lovely realm, a kingdom so holy and so fair. Now the blow which pride received on the awful tree of Calvary's mount, the humility forged by the Son of God, were of such immeasurable depths, that (this being now the warp and woof of Heaven's very life) sin can never again lift its ugly head. The cross of Christ brought in a new order of things for all the universe.

45

THE CROSS —
THE THEOLOGY OF HEAVEN

IT FELL TO ME TO SPEAK to the students of a seminary where it was taboo to mention the blood of Christ. These high-browed intellectuals who gloried in their advanced theological concepts had long since left behind such antiquated concepts, which may have obtained for primitive Christians, but who would think of imposing them upon such cultured, philosophical, highly trained men as they?

Well, in my simplicity, being of another opinion, I concluded that my brethren needed to be taught. So my theme was, "The Theology of Heaven." It provoked considerable attention. Imagine, this "seedy missionary," just in from the sticks, pretending to know what the theology of Heaven is. Why, we haven't yet made sure just what the theology of earth ought to be.

It was all very simple. It was found, so I ventured to point out, in the Song of the Redeemed as recorded by John in the Apocalypse. "Worthy art thou, O Lamb of God, for thou wast slain, and hast redeemed us to God by thy blood. These are they which came out of great tribulation, and have washed their robes, and made them white in the blood of the Lamb" (Revelation 5:12 and 7:14).

It was brief. I hardly needed to point out that in Heaven the hosts of the redeemed could see nothing so wonderful as the cross of Christ, nor could they find anything a millionth part so precious as the blood of Christ, nor was it possible to conceive of aught so amazing, so altogether blessed in which to glory as the achievement of the Son of God on Calvary, by which we are saved. Christ-centered, cross-centered was the theology of Heaven, where unnumbered multitudes sing of the never-ending virtues of the blood of Christ.

It struck home. The Holy Spirit used it to pierce proud hearts and there was fruit which after many years still abides, and rich fellowship with choice souls still preaching the Word and magnifying Christ the Lord and His redeeming cross, was the result.

A more enthralling scene than what we have in Revelation could not be imagined. "I beheld," says John, "and, lo, a great multitude, which no man could number, of all nations, and kindreds, and people, and tongues, stood before the throne, and before the Lamb, clothed with white robes, and palms in their hands; and cried with a loud voice, saying, Salvation to our God which sitteth upon the throne, and unto the Lamb. And all the angels stood round about the throne . . . and fell before the throne on their faces, and worshipped God, saying, Amen: Blessing, and glory, and wisdom, and thanksgiving, and honour, and power, and might, be unto our God for ever and ever. Amen" (Revelation 7:9-12).

We must quote the entire passage, it is so enthralling. "And one of the elders," the apostle John goes on to say, "answered, saying unto me, What are these which are arrayed in white robes? and whence came they?" Now the answer is most revealing, beautifully in accord with the theme of these chapters dedicated as they are to the cross of Christ. It is most significant that the answer is not, "Why, these are the great saints of the Church who by their labors and achievements earned the right to enter into. Heaven's glory. These are the missionaries who suffered untold privations for the cause of Christ. These are the faithful preachers who labored incessantly that Christ might be made known. These are the monks who wore hair shirts, lacerated their bodies, and fasted day and night. Or these are they who separated themselves from the world and refused to fellowship with sinners.

The answer is overwhelmingly significant. "These are they which came out of great tribulation [who that is a Christian does not come out of great tribulation?], and have washed their robes, and made them white in the blood of the Lamb" (Revelation 7:13, 14).

Perhaps you feel inclined to get around this which is not pleasing to "the flesh," ever eager to find some good in itself in which to glory, by saying, "Oh, but this is only symbolism." Yes. But the matter cannot be brushed off in this fashion. For even when we admit that symbolism is involved, the central fact of all the Scriptures still holds. This central fact is none other than that the Son of God wrought redemption on Calvary's cross, bearing the sins of the world, this being the sinner's hope, and the ground of his eternal felicity.

We are not saying that good works and a genuine Christian walk do not have a place nor that they are no requirement. But they are the fruits of the Christian life, never the ground, or shall I say the procuring cause of the believer's security and acceptance with God. He is accepted in the Beloved (see Ephesians 1:6). His robes "have been washed and made white in the blood of the Lamb." Or, if you wish, He has been redeemed by the Crucified-Risen Lord, who bore his sins on the accursed tree.

John goes on to affirm, yea, to clinch the matter, saying: "Therefore are they before the throne of God, and serve him day and night in his temple: and he that sitteth on the throne shall dwell among them. They shall hunger no more, neither thirst any more; neither shall the sun light on them, nor any heat. For the Lamb which is in the midst of the throne shall feed them, and shall lead them unto living fountains of waters: and God shall wipe away all tears from their eyes" (7:15-17).

If such words do not move you not only to desire but actually to come to the fountain filled with blood drawn from Immanuel's veins, so that plunged beneath that flood you may lose all your guilty stains (if I may speak in terms of the immortal hymn), then, of course, further pleadings from me would be useless. What folly to add to such a revelation of the efficacy of the cross and the glory of the redeemed.

The Lamb which Abraham told Isaac centuries before would be given, has been wondrously provided. The precious blood of the "Lamb slain" has lost none of its cleansing, redeeming efficacy. It is still a fact that to enter in through the gates of the Holy City to be forever with the Lord, we must wash our garments and make them white in the blood of the Lamb: in other words, the cross of Christ, in which God exhausted His love, and wisdom, and mercy, and power in order to redeem sinful men, is our only hope.

46

VICTORY THROUGH THE CROSS

WE ARE LIVING in a day of unprecedented oppression. Many feel that John's word in Revelation 12, where he says that the enemy would come with great wrath, knowing that his time is short, is approaching if not already upon us. Ephesians 6, with its call to battle inasmuch as we wrestle not with flesh and blood but with principalities and powers, against the rulers of the darkness of this world, is God's watchword for such an hour as this.

Revelation 12 throws abundant light upon the present world situation, with its ever present threat of a third World War, and the despair of millions under the heel of Communism. Needless to say, the prophetic aspect will not be discussed. We are dealing with the supreme underlying principle of the entire body of revelation as found in the Sacred Scriptures. Nowhere is it more in evidence than here in Revelation 12.

John says there was war in Heaven. Now there has been war ever since the rebellion of the great angelic prince, who drew a third part of the angels of Heaven with him, took place. Two thrones are at war, God's and Satan's.

We have already dwelt upon the fact that the purpose of the coming of the Son of God was to destroy the works of Satan (I John 3:8), and that this could only be done in a way consonant with the righteous character of God. Not by a divine "fiat," but by a just fulfillment of God's law broken by sinful men. This was accomplished through the cross of Christ, where all ground for Satanic accusation (he is the accuser of the brethren who accused them day and night before our God, Revelation

12:10) was taken away in a righteous fashion, the law having exhausted its just claims in the death of the Son of God.

"Now is come salvation," writes John, "and strength, and the kingdom of our God, and the power of his Christ: for the accuser of our brethren is cast down . . ." (Revelation 12:10). Ah, the wondrous fashion, immeasurably praiseworthy, in perfect keeping with the character of our thrice holy God, by which the awful accuser, as he pointed to a broken law and slandered the Most High for passing over its demands in His providential care of sinful man, was silenced. The cross will forever tell the story.

Now this glorious achievement of the Son of God, who, as we read in Colossians 2:14, spoiled principalities and powers (the principalities of hell) and made a show of them openly, triumphing over them by means of His cross, gives to those who own Christ as Saviour and Lord a mighty weapon. Before the believer, invested with the authority which is his in view of his oneness with his triumphant Lord, to whom all authority has been given in Heaven and upon earth, the prince of this world cannot stand. All legal ground, as we have just seen, has been cut from beneath his feet. The devil, in brief, is a defeated foe whose rights have all been annulled. He knows it and can do nothing but "give up," or, if you prefer, "take hands off and flee," when the believer declares him to be such.

The great Scriptural affirmation as regards all this is Revelation 12: "They [the brethren] overcame him [the dragon, the roaring lion of I Peter 5:8] by the blood of the Lamb, and by the word of their testimony; and they loved not their lives unto the death. Therefore rejoice, ye heavens . . ." (Revelation 12:11, 12).

So we have come afresh and in a new way to the cross of Christ. "They overcame him by the blood of the Lamb." By what other means would they find the courage and the faith to face the "Goliath" of this world and make him "bite the dust" in ignominious defeat? In these awful conflicts with the prince of this world, which the soldiers of Christ must endure, no other weapon avails.

Woe to the soldier who falls back upon his theology, his Biblical knowledge, his churchly position and honors, his good works, his self-righteousness. The devil, as many to their woe and shame are learning, can tear all this to shreds. Self-right-eousness, whatever its form is but a toy pistol before the on-slaughts, the awful bombardments of the dragon and his hosts. Even so righteous a man as Job could not withstand the fiery blasts from hell and its prince. His self-righteousness had to go to the wall. Ah yes, he did at last triumph, for he knew that his Redeemer liveth and would stand on the earth and accomplish His redeeming work.

But this is not all. John says, in effect, that they overcame because of the word of their testimony. What does this mean? It means that we must appropriate by faith and declare the enemy a defeated foe, else he will be as mighty as ever. He is still the roaring lion walking about seeking whom he may de-vour. He only flees when faced with a determined: "In the name of Jesus, get hence, your rights were annulled at Calvary." We must give the command of faith. "Whosoever shall say unto this mountain, Be thou removed and be thou cast into the sea (moun-tain of Satanic oppression); and shall not doubt in his heart, but shall believe that those things which he saith shall come to pass; he shall have whatsoever he saith" (Mark 11:23).

I have a friend who puts it this way. He is at the head of a great business enterprise. Someone came to him to demand payment on a certain debt. He says he told the gentleman that the debt was already paid. But the gentleman became violent and assumed a threatening attitude against which my friend took a yet more determined stand, producing the bill with its official stamp, "Paid." My friend said he was obliged to literally poke the paper in the man's face and say, "Look at this; now get out of here."

My friend, who is a Christian, tells me that that is the way he faces the devil. He orders him to look at the cross where all his sins were dealt with, where all ground given was legally removed, and to flee. The result is that the enemy flees. That is a Christian businessman's way of casting the "mountain" into the sea. The enemy can stand before all else. He cannot stand before the cross of Christ where the great debt of sin was for-ever liquidated.

But there is a final point. John says that they (the brethren) loved not their lives unto the death. What does this mean? Here again we are taken to the cross. Not only was all legal ground removed from Satan at Calvary; the old creation (the old man, the life of the fallen Adam, the principle of pride) was also terminated. There is an affinity between Satan and the old nature with its pride and self-love. You cannot overcome him if you are not willing to take God's verdict regarding the old creation as expressed in Romans 6, where we are told that "the old man" was crucified together with Christ; for the life of nature with its pride will give him ground on which to stand. Paul's "I am crucified with Christ . . . . It is no longer I but Christ," is the only safe ground. Have you taken it? If not, take it now, and be more than conqueror through Him who loved you.

47

WHAT ARE THESE WOUNDS?

AT THE CENTER of the Apocalypse is the Lamb as it had been slain. Over and over we come upon this tender title by which the Lord Jesus Christ is made known. Some of the references are incomplete; it is the Lamb, nothing more. But it is understood that it is the Lamb, slain. In the thirteenth chapter He is heralded as the Lamb slain from the foundation of the world. Needless to say, it is the One John the Baptist proclaimed, beholding Him in His sacrificial character taking away the sins of the world.

A great change has come: the cross, death, the tomb, resurrection, ascension, glorification have wrought mighty transformations. He is now in the throne. But the Lamb who, when taken to the slaughter, as said the prophet Isaiah, opened not His mouth, has not returned to the glory which was His with the Father before the world was, without taking with Him the fruits of His victory. All authority is now His, both in Heaven and upon earth. The Name given Him is above every name that is named, not only in this world, but also in that which is to come (Ephesians 1:21).

Of course it is all symbolic. These verities are so great, they could be stated in no other way. The Saviour is no Lamb; we understand. Why, He upholds all things by the word of His power (Hebrews 1:3). However, had it been possible to find a more fitting figure, we may be sure the Holy Spirit, who moved the sacred writers, would have employed it. It is the Lamblike character of our blessed Redeemer, stooping from such heights to go all the way to Calvary's cross, which in the Apocalypse is ever before us. The Lamb slain from the foundation of the world

(Revelation 13:8) is our Lord's official name in view of His masterpiece, the taking away of the sins of the world on the cross of Calvary. In the Name, the Person and the Sacrifice are one. No other title so befits Him now in glory and in the midst of the throne as this one, for our Lord is now and forever will be the Crucified-Risen King.

He can be known in no other fashion, by which I mean to say that if we would know Jesus without the wounds which befell Him at Calvary, our hope is vain. Unless, of course, as many today are, we would be satisfied with a false Christ. The false Christ of the "isms" and cults has no wounds. It is so comfortable to have a false Christ (that is why Satan has no trouble foisting them upon men). For the false Christ does not appear to me with scars inflicted by my sin, and also removed thereby.

He, Christ Jesus our Lord, came one way and went back to Heaven and the throne another. He came as God (all things were made by Him; God was manifest in the flesh, I Timothy 3:16). He returned to His throne a Man. He is now and will forever be the God-Man. "Jesus Christ the same yesterday, and to day, and for ever" (Hebrews 13:8). In that glorified human body the marks of the cross will forever be within the plain view of the angelic hosts and the unnumbered saints who have washed their robes and made them white in the blood of the Lamb.

"What are these wounds in thine hands?" the prophet Zechariah portrays Israel as saying to the Lord upon the occasion of His Coming. Then shall He answer, "Those with which I was wounded in the house of my friends. They shall look upon me whom they have pierced." The redeemed in Heaven will not need to ask, "What are these wounds?" But for them, the offense is gone. They sing: "Worthy art thou, O Lamb of God, for thou wast slain and hast redeemed us to God by thy blood."

I am not following any particular order or being concerned about the prophetic aspect of the Apocalypse. There are those who are equipped to decipher its wondrous mysteries. For the present I can see nothing else but the never-to-be-fully-fathomed glory of "the Lamb as though it had been slain." Nothing so enthralling in Heaven or on earth, in time or eternity.

However, we must now face up to a word in Revelation 6

which I wish we might pass over. But no, it must be looked squarely in the eye, as we say. It is that upon our Lord's return according to the promise, many shall seek to hide themselves in the dens and in the rocks of the mountains, saying, "Fall on us, and hide us from the face of him that sitteth on the throne, and from the wrath of the Lamb: for the great day of his wrath is come; and who shall be able to stand?" (Revelation 6:16, 17).

Now it is not the blood of the Lamb, but the wrath of the Lamb. I feared I would have a difficult time interpreting this. But as it appears to me now there is really no problem. The Saviour, so lovely, yea, infinitely adorable, could not be without wrath, for such a one could not hate sin which is immeasurably hateful.

If He could look upon sin without experiencing a righteous, holy indignation, He would be less than good men I have known who could not look upon injustice, abuses, the outrage of innocent childhood, the raping of lovely maidens by brutal soldiers, the infamous crimes of a tyrant such as Hitler, without revulsion, and fearful anger. This is the One who could say to the Pharisees who made long prayers and yet devoured widows' houses, "Ye generation of vipers, how shall ye escape the damnation of hell?" (Matthew 23:33).

A preacher once said, the wrath of the Lamb is love that has been spurned. Be that as it may, *this* which sounds so contrary to Him who was moved with such compassion as He looked upon the multitudes, "sheep without a shepherd," and who drew to Himself fallen women, lepers, publicans, sitting with sinners at banquets, saying to the thief on a cross by His side, "Verily I say unto thee, To day shalt thou be with me in paradise," is something as certain and as inevitable as the forgiveness which springs from this same Lamb slain for sinners. Were the cost of the sacrifice made to free men from guilt, less, then less certain would be the doom of those who spurn God's infinitely gracious offer of salvation made through His Son. That is to say, if the cross does not save, then, of course, sin's retribution is only enhanced by the very gift whose purpose is to free.

Infinite Love, spurned as it seeks to redeem the sinner by such a passionate willingness to bear all his shame, and guilt, and sin, even as it was when the Saviour went down into the awful abyss of darkness and death wounded for man's transgression, smitten on the cross for man's iniquities — infinite Love, I repeat, spurned by those it would save at so great a cost, becomes, as it rightly should, wrath. What would you say of a son who spurned his father's love, having gone to the gallows to die in his stead? Would not all peoples cry "Shame!" at such a one, and be moved by holy anger? Wrath is as right and needful as love. If we will not embrace a Saviour, we shall be compelled to meet a Judge.

48

THE LAMB SLAIN —
FROM THE FOUNDATION OF THE WORLD

IN CHAPTER 13 of the book of Revelation
the apostle tells of the perilous times that are to come, before
the appearing of our Lord and Saviour Jesus Christ and the
consummation of His great work in the establishment of His
kingdom. First there is the political beast rising out of the sea,
to whom the dragon gives power, speaking great things and
blasphemous, and making war on the saints and overcoming
them — power over all kindreds, and tongues, and nations. And
second, the ecclesiastical beast, which had the appearance of
a lamb, but spoke as a dragon, and which wrought great wonders
and miracles, deceiving them that dwell on the earth, with
power even to give life to an image —— the image of the political
beast.

As has been said, our aim is not to interpret these matters.
We shall take them simply in their setting in relation to the central fact of the chapter (central as we are seeing to all the Scriptures). It is that though, as is written, all that dwell upon the
earth shall worship the beast and receive his mark, there will
be those who shall overcome this awful pressure emanating
from the pit and refuse to worship him. It will be those whose
names are written in "the book of life of the Lamb slain from
the foundation of the world" (Revelation 13:8).

Let us get at the basic facts at once, apart from all prophecy
and symbolism. One wonders, at times, if perhaps we are not
moving rapidly into at least the shadow of the Great Tribulation.
Great historical events cast their shadows before becoming a

178

fact. Even now there are ungodly political powers being un-leashed which threaten to bring all the world under their sway. And woe unto him who refuses to worship their image and re-ceive their mark. Millions can bear witness to this fact. Some of the testimonies you read of those who have withstood "the beast," preferring torture and death (should it come) rather than receive its "mark," make your blood run cold, and you cry, "May God deliver us."

Be all that as it may, there is a universal setting to all this. This world in which Christ was crucified, since man's fall into sin, has been a "beast." Paul, in writing to the Galatians, says that Christ gave Himself that He might deliver us from this present *evil* world. We have an exact photograph of its ungodly image at Calvary. You say, but the Jews did this. The reply is, yes, but sin as such has ever done *that*. The spirit of the world with its pride and worship of Mammon still does *that*. Paul says that the mind of "the flesh" (self-life) is enmity toward God. Look at the cross and you will no longer harbor doubts.

John puts it even stronger here in Revelation 13, where he says that the Lamb was slain from the foundation of the world. Ah, if I but had wisdom to declare the meaning of this most amazing affirmation of the Scripture. May we not say, in any case, that it points to the fact that, far back, even since the hour of man's rebellion, the cross was a fact in the loving heart of God, to become so at last in time, and in history. God being as He is, and sin being what it is, it could not be otherwise.

There are those who feel that not only since the rebellion of man, but rather from the hour when the great Cherubim, Son of the Morning, Lucifer, drew off the third part of the angelic host into a wicked revolt in defiance of the government of God, the cross was a potential fact in the loving economy of God. Oh, the suffering for One who loves as only God can. Indeed, it could not have been otherwise, God being as He is, and sin on the part of celestial beings what it was and is.

We have seen how that the cross of Christ was not only for the expiation of man's guilt and his reconciliation to God, but that the prince of darkness (yea, and of this world) might be judged and order brought into a universe "topsy-turvy" be-cause of rebellion in the celestial realms. See John 16, verse 11, where we read that it is one of the functions of the Holy Spirit to convince believers that Satan has already been judged; and also Revelation 12 where we are told that Hallelujah's fill Heaven with joy unspeakable because that old serpent, called the Devil, and Satan and his angels have been cast out — "neither was their place found any more in heaven." Such was the victory wrought on Calvary (Hebrews 2:14; also Colossians 2:14, 15).

But we must return to our main thesis. Multitudes, John tells us, were unable to stand before the "beast," worshiping him and receiving in their foreheads his mark. It is so even now. How many there are who fail to overcome the world and who bow before her taboos, and spirit, and fashion in total servitude. They do indeed receive her mark.

John says, however, that those whose names are written in the book of life of "the Lamb slain from the foundation of the world" shall not be overcome. The great promises the Saviour makes to the churches (see chapters two and three of Revelation, "he that overcometh I will give to eat of the tree of life which is in the midst of the paradise of God") are all and only for overcomers.

And how do we overcome? Through the cross. We overcome even as the Saviour overcame. Here is the key. The overcomers have their names written in the book of life of the Lamb slain. We can overcome, in a word, only as we stand united by faith with the Crucified-Risen Lord.

"To him that overcometh I will grant to sit with me in my throne, even as I overcame, and am set down with my Father in his throne" (Revelation 3:21).

49

THE SON OF GOD GOES FORTH TO WAR

THERE IS A NOBLE HYMN of the Church we seldom sing. Its title is, "The Son of God Goes Forth to War." Perhaps many have felt that the martial spirit of the hymn does not really represent the meek and lowly Jesus who stooped to wash the feet of fishermen. I wonder if we have failed to fully interpret the Son of God.

One of the tricks of Communism today is to talk peace as if war were an unworthy business, and so disarm the free nations (were it possible). Something similar has been happening to the Church. I wonder who is behind this demilitarizing the Christian movement, which is no longer a mighty crusade? But it *is* warfare. If we do not believe it, the prince of this world certainly does. He is on the warpath as never before in all history, for he knows his time is short.

I rejoice that I may leave questions of prophecy with those who are equipped to deal with such matters. My task is to stick to the deep, underlying principle of the Scriptures to which they bear witness, namely the victory of the cross, the triumph of the Crucified-Risen Lord.

There seems to be a variety of opinions as regards the four horses of the Apocalypse. Many feel that the first, a white horse whose rider, crowned, goes forth conquering and to conquer, represents the Risen, Ascended Christ, the extension of whose Kingdom shall have no end.

However, as regards the white horse and its rider of chapter 19, there can be no doubt. He is called Faithful and True, and in righteousness doth judge and make war. We read that his eyes are as a flame of fire and that on his head are many crowns. He has a name which no one knows but himself. He is clothed with a vesture *dipped in blood*. Furthermore, should anyone harbor doubts as to his identity, the apostle adds a final word which leaves no room for further uncertainty. His name is called the Word of God.

Oh, the glory of this scene; the Son of God is followed by the armies of Heaven upon white horses, clothed in linen, white and clean. Out of his mouth goes a sharp sword that with it He could smite the nations, for He shall rule them with a rod of iron. Should there remain a slight uncertainty in spite of all that has been said, and a doubt should still remain that it could possibly be the Compassionate Lord Jesus, the Christ of God, John gives a final proof saying that He has on His vesture, and on His thigh a name written, King of kings and Lord of lords.

This is the amazing revelation of our Lord and Saviour Jesus Christ as we come to the closing chapters of the Apocalypse. What does it mean? It means, apart from all questions of prophecy, that the One who died on Calvary's cross and on the third day rose again, will, as it were, have the last word in the great struggle the saints are obliged to carry on with the evil one.

There are hidden forces of evil which behind the scenes of social, political, ideological, and racial clashes, behind the "cold war" that is straining and draining the nations to the very hilt, behind all wickedness whatever its form, for which there is no promise of mercy. According to the revelations of the Sacred Scriptures the devil and his angels are to be cast at last into a lake of fire.

The enemy has been judged, stripped of the legal rights man's sin had given him, but the roaring lion of I Peter 5:8, for reasons no doubt beyond our ken found only in the inscrutable councils of God, is still stalking the earth with his cohorts. For these there is no promise of mercy, Papini notwithstanding. The Italian writer thinks that Satan himself will at last be converted from the error of his way. But the Lord in His Word speaks otherwise. Satan did his worst at Calvary (where the Lord did His best) and we are told that he will never go back on that. That is settled for all eternity.

No, it will be war until the end. The false prophets cried, "Peace, peace," but there was no peace. Ephesians 6, Paul's description of the Church's great struggle where Christians are called to war as soldiers of Christ, is the divine analysis of what is taking place. We are told to buckle on the armor of God and enter the lists with the devil.

The armies of Heaven follow the Great Captain; so do we. Away with the pusillanimous prattle of our day. We are soldiers and an all-out conflict is on. The Salvation Army is right. It is War. We can never strike too hard, nor fight too valiantly, nor hate too intensely. ("Ye that love the Lord, hate evil," Psalm 97:10), as we wage war against the devil and his hosts.

And there is nothing to fear. We follow the One who has never lost a battle. All authority has been given unto Him in Heaven and upon earth. His vesture drips with blood. The Scriptures never let us lose sight of the cross, for it was victory. The hosts of hell have been judged. Through death our heavenly Captain destroyed him who had the power of death, that is to say the devil. The great angelic prince who was routed in the desert and finally had his head bruised at Calvary where principalities and powers were spoiled, and made a show of openly (Colossians 2:14, 15), has been reduced to an utter zero status in the economy of God. So let the soldiers of the cross take heart. They must realize that they advance in the strength of a victory already consummated.

The armies of Heaven follow the crowned One on the white charger whose vesture is dipped in blood. And we still here below, where the awful conflict of the ages is coming to its great Waterloo, is fast approaching its final throes, must keep our eyes upon the Heavenly Captain, King of kings and Lord of lords. With Him we do not press toward a possible victory. The victory has already been won, and we stand in victory.

Only let us remember that our Prince won through death. The cross was His weapon as it must be ours. That is the meaning of His vesture dipped in blood. He is still the Crucified though He be Risen. We are defeated apart from a never ending identification with the cross. For if the devil can get us away from the cross, the old self-life lifts its ugly head afresh and this gives "ground" to the enemy. He can plant his foot on the "old self-life" and claim it.

We follow in the wake of the One crowned whose vesture is dipped in blood — more than conquerors through Him who loved us.

50

THE MARRIAGE SUPPER OF THE LAMB

THE BIBLE COMES to a close with the most stupendous prospect of all the ages. It opens with man fresh from the hands of God in a garden crowned with unspeakable glory and riches, falling into sin and death. It closes with redeemed man reunited with the One he had so offended, his Father and God, in what is called the Marriage Supper of the Lamb.

That is to say, he owes it to the Lamb that was slain. He is there in the midst of the splendors of Heaven because of the immeasurable virtue of the cross. He has not come by any merit or virtue of his own. His robes, as we have already seen, have been washed in the blood of the Lamb. Heaven knows of nothing so wonderful as earth's highest glory which is the cross of Christ.

"The marriage supper of the Lamb is come, let us be glad and rejoice and give honour to him" (Revelation 19:7). His bride, we are told, has made herself ready for to her was granted that she should be arrayed in fine linen, clean and white. The fine linen, says the apostle, is the righteousness of the saints.

Little wonder that the Seer of Patmos should write: "And I heard as it were the voice of a great multitude, and as the voice of many waters, and as the voice of mighty thunderings, saying, Alleluia: for the Lord God omnipotent reigneth. . . . And he saith unto me, Write, Blessed are they which are called unto the marriage supper of the Lamb" (Revelation 19:6, 9).

Perhaps there are those among my gracious readers who

may be inclined to lift their eyebrows and with an incredulous shrug, retort, saying, "Oh, but this is all symbolical." Of course it is. Almost everything in the Apocalypse is such. However, this only adds to the glory of the Central Fact. Would it be possible to couch the matchless glory of the eternal union of the redeemed with their infinitely adorable Redeemer, in a oneness of spirit so deep that Jesus our Lord Himself in the days of His humiliation declared that it was such a union as existed between Him and the Father (see John 17), in terms more fitting or more expressive than that of marriage?

This figure runs all through the Scriptures. The Old Testament is full of it. That great song, the greatest ever written, therefore entitled The Song of Songs, in which the spouse (the Church, the bride) cries, "I am my beloved's and my beloved is mine," is the supreme Biblical expression of this fact. It was forever flashing forth in the Saviour's parables and words. "Can the children of the bridechamber fast while the bridegroom is with them?" was His answer to the Pharisees who could not understand why the disciples of Jesus did not fast. At the marriage feast at Cana of Galilee where the Saviour most appropriately turned water into wine so that no shadow might mar the feast, we plainly observe that our Lord saw in this most beautiful ceremony a picture of His own great purpose at last to be consummated in what John speaks of as "the marriage supper of the Lamb." His hour, so He spoke to Mary, had not yet come.

But now, the apostle tells us in Revelation chapter 19, the marriage supper of the Lamb is come. Were I to be invited to Buckingham Palace to be the guest of the queen at the marriage feast of a beloved son, I would, of course, be expected to conform most scrupulously not only to the etiquette of the court, but to every wish the queen might make known as regards the occasion. If I were to go unkempt and in overalls, I would deserve to have the door shut in my face and to be kicked off the royal premises.

Now as regards the marriage supper of the Lamb, the manner, and dress, and etiquette, and all are to be found in one word. John the Baptist said when first he looked upon Jesus: "Behold the Lamb of God, which taketh away the sin of the world." Abraham said it when to Isaac he declared: "God will provide a Lamb for the sacrifice." John uttered that all-inclusive word when he said that in the midst of the throne he beheld a Lamb as though it had been slain. Indeed, it is all in the one great word — a Lamb slain. In other words, the cross of Christ. Oh, how it shines forth from the wounds ever fresh of the Crucified-Risen-Ascended-Enthroned Lord, the Christ of God.

May I quote a passage from *The Lion Lamb* by D. M. Panton?:

> The crowning worthiness Heaven puts upon Christ is due to Calvary. All the splendid attributes, all the incomparable glories, concentrate in the wounds. The place of a Lamb is upon an altar, but, because of a perfect atonement perfectly accepted, the Lamb is now upon the Throne. The wounds abide. It is, as it were, a fresh death, for the atonement can never lose its freshness. God never forgets it, the angels never forget it, the redeemed never forget it. Eternal wounds are the pledge of an eternal pardon. The man who knows the incarnate God slain for human sin, stands at the innermost core of truth, and knows heaven's final secret. . . . Christ was slain prospectively from the foundation of the world. He was slain typically in a thousand sacrifices under the Law, He was slain judicially by the pre-determined counsel of God, He was slain actually by Jew and Gentile, He is slain retrospectively by every trampler on the Blood. "Thou did'st purchase unto God with thy blood, men of every tribe, and tongue, and people, and nation." The Blood alone purchases the sinner to God. The Father comes into his inheritance of human souls only by the blood of His Son. Therefore what do all angels yield to the Lamb? "The power, and riches, and wisdom, and might, and honour, and glory, and blessing!" What a song! All crowns meet upon that brow, all power is in those pierced hands, all love flows from that rent side, all the Godhead shines in that face. This is the theology of all the angels of God.

But there is even yet deeper meaning to be plumbed. "Blessed are they which are called unto the marriage supper of the Lamb." It is the union of God's redeemed people with the Lamb for all eternity. But how can I come into a vital, indissoluble, ever-lastingly perfect union with my Saviour the Lord Jesus Christ, who is and forever most essentially will be the Crucified-Risen Lord (John says in the midst of the throne a Lamb as though it had been slain) if I am not willing to share His cross, and with Paul say, "I am crucified together with Christ; it is no longer I, but Christ liveth in me"?

It is the marriage supper of the *Lamb*. It is, in a word, the cross which forever secures Heaven and safeguards the Holy City of God, whose streets are of gold, against any further appearance of evil.

51

THE RIVER OF WATER OF LIFE

IT SURPRISES NO ONE that the Bible should close, as it does in the twenty-second chapter of the Apocalypse, with a vision of the stream of blessing which the apostle designates as "a pure river of water of life, clear as crystal, proceeding out of the throne of God and of the Lamb." Through sin came death. But Christ the Lord abolished the awful reign of death (death even while men seem to live) bringing life and immortality to light through the Gospel as we have it in II Timothy 1:10.

Life, life, life, this was the Redeemer's object as He came to restore what man had lost through sin; rivers of living water flowing from his innermost being, as it is in John 7:38. But the invitation seems to be yet more emphatic, free from all conditions save a willingness to come, as it is found on the lips of the Risen Lord here in the closing words of the Sacred Scriptures. Could anything more in keeping with man's deepest need, yea, his eternal blessedness, his unending felicity be conceived?

"I Jesus have sent mine angel to testify unto you these things in the churches. I am the root and offspring of David, and the bright and morning star. And the Spirit and the bride say, Come. And let him that heareth say, Come. And let him that is athirst come. And whosoever will, let him take the water of life freely" (Revelation 22:16, 17).

How it stirs one to see the Lord Christ, the Head of the Church, blast away all barriers, tear down all ecclesiastical walls, and annihilate all that law and sin have put in the sinner's way. Say what you will, object as you may, preach whatever you please, still it stands written, and it is the Saviour Himself who speaks. He solemnly declares that there is but one condition, one and only one prerequisite. It is a willingness to *come*. I seem to hear voices, frantically exclaiming: "But you must repent first." My answer is, there is no repentance so effective and so pleasing to God as just plain coming to Jesus. If there be those who feel that they must make the "coming" less easy by linking it up with ecclesiastical requirements, they are free to do so. But Christ Jesus, the Lord and Head of the Church, lays down no condition save one — a willingness to come. The river flows freely. It flows everlastingly for all who will come.

Now having said this, we must face up to the fact that the river of water of life, clear as crystal, flows from the throne of God, and of the Lamb. John the apostle has already told us that in the midst of the throne stands "a Lamb as it had been slain" (Revelation 5:6). This does away with all fear that the way to the river may be lightly taken. If barriers are needed, they are all here. The river of water of life proceeds from the Lamb. To this goal God was marching all down the ages. History finds here the key to unlock its mysteries. The Lamb was slain from the foundation of the world (Revelation 13:8).

I repeat, if further conditions are needed, here they are. When the Roman soldier pierced the Redeemer's breast, "forthwith came there out blood and water" (John 19:34). Now here in the Apocalypse it is the same John writing; and most emphatically let it be said, it is the same stream flowing. "There is a fountain filled with blood drawn from Immanuel's veins," and it is still true that "sinners plunged beneath that flood lose all their guilty stains." So we are led to observe that the one great condition is not too easy after all. It runs, as we have seen, straight through the Bible.

It was expressed in Abel's sacrifice. Isaiah's "And the Lord laid on him the iniquity of us all," bears witness. "He is brought," says the prophet, "as a lamb to the slaughter, and as a sheep before her shearers is dumb, so he openeth not his mouth" (Isaiah 53:6, 7). No one saw it more clearly than John the Baptist, when on that memorable day he cried, "Behold the Lamb of God, that taketh away the sin of the world." Paul could find nothing greater to say than just this: "But God commendeth his love toward us, in that, while we were yet sinners, Christ died for us. . . . For if when we were enemies, we were reconciled to God by the death of his Son, much more, being reconciled, we shall be saved by his life."

So let us do away with our fears. It is the "Lamb Slain" who invites us to come. It is from the wounded breast (pierced by an unnumbered billion spears of sin and shame) of the infinitely adorable Saviour of mankind, Jesus Christ the Lord, that the river flows. The moment you approach the river of water of life, clear as crystal, you are acknowledging your sin and need, for the river flows from the cross where Christ was slain to put away the sins of the world.

Then, too, this life is very pure ("a pure river of water of life, clear as crystal"), and as you drink you are made pure. It is the life of the Crucified, and as you partake you "eat of the flesh and drink of the blood" (see John 6:54) of the Son of God, and this is the life of the ages, in which there is no vain pride, nor love of self, nor unholy thing. So let us heed the Saviour's call. He cannot say it more emphatically, or more tenderly. He sweeps away all barriers and says: "Whosoever will, let him take the water of life freely."

It is with difficulty that one refrains from fervent Hallelujah's, for here is the fulfillment of that most agonzing cry which issues from the sin-stricken breast of man, vainly seeking to quench his thirst for "Life" by feeding on earth's empty baubles. Moses struck the rock and water gushed forth for Israel's famishing multitudes. The psalmist could find no more expressive manner with which to make known his joy: "How excellent is thy lovingkindness, O God! therefore the children of men put their trust under the shadow of thy wings. They shall be abundantly satisfied with the fatness of thy house; and thou shalt make them drink of the river of thy pleasures" (Psalm 36:7,8). And in Psalm 46:4 we are told that "there is a river, the streams whereof shall make glad the city of God." Ezekiel the prophet saw a river emanating from beneath the altar (in the Bible the only legitimate altar is the cross of Christ whereof all others were types), waters to the ankles, waters to the knees, waters to the thighs, waters that could be passed only by swimming. "And it shall come to pass, that everything that liveth, which moveth, whithersoever the rivers shall come, shall live: and there shall be a very great multitude of fish" (Ezekiel 47:9).

Oh, that the children of men might plunge in and live. All the doors of God's mercy are open, so let us come. The cross of Christ has removed all the barriers of sin and pride, and guilt and shame, so let us come and drink freely of the water of life, and having drunk, drink again, and forevermore. Amen.